RUN WITH THE
CHEETAHS

Jerry Freishtat

New York | Los Angeles | London | Sydney

ISBN Softcover: 978-1-63792-697-0
ISBN Hardcover: 978-1-63792-701-4

To my five children,

As I sit down to pen these words, my heart swells with love and gratitude for the incredible blessing you are in my life. From the moment you entered this world, you brought immeasurable joy, laughter, and meaning to my existence. Each day spent with you is a precious gift filled with unforgettable moments.

This dedication is to express the depth of my commitment and devotion as your father. You are the stars that illuminate the darkest nights and the compass that guides me through life's journey. Your unique personalities, dreams, and accomplishments fill me with immense pride, and I am in awe of the remarkable individuals you have become. Each of you has grown to be your own type of warrior. Your serenity will always be my greatest aspiration, and your well-being my constant concern.

May your lives be filled with love, purpose, challenges, and fulfillment. You are my greatest legacy, and I am endlessly grateful for the privilege of being your father. You are my proudest achievement in life!

With all my love,
Dad

TABLE OF CONTENTS

FOREWORD
BY RUSSELL ANDERSON

Congratulations, Dear Reader!

You have found your way to a most remarkable book!

This book's many lessons are a gift from the author to all of us seeking a better life. Inside these pages, you will find hundreds of actionable ideas, concepts, themes, and stories that will teach and propel you to create your own better life and, step-by-step-by-step, your own amazing future! And you can start today. You simply cannot beat that.

Let's begin right here:

"Do the best you can until you KNOW better.

Then, when you know better, DO better."

These are very wise words credited to world-renowned author, poet, and activist Maya Angelou – and it's all here within these pages.

Building a successful life is absolutely a Do-It-Yourself job because you are NOT going to learn this within the traditional educational channels. Sadly, it is simply not taught.

Every bit of research says almost all of us sell ourselves short – we accomplish only a fraction of what we are truly capable of – why is that?

Once again, it's WHAT WE KNOW – and WHAT WE DO.

So, ultimately, what you will need to succeed is TWO THINGS -

1) the knowledge of WHAT TO DO, and -

2) the WILL to DO IT.

And again - it's all here in this wonderful book.

Let me ask you, how does someone with nothing become someone with everything?

Picture this - a man loses everything: all his worldly possessions, all his money, his family, his business. And standing next to this man is a second man - with the exact same circumstances.

The first man goes on and rebuilds his business, his family, and his fortune. The second man remains stuck. Stuck with his minimal lot in life, losing hope for his dreams of success and finally settling for far less than he is capable of becoming. Why?

I have lived and pondered this question for decades and have never seen a better example of this played out IRL (in real life) as when I was friend, witness, and observer of THIS AUTHOR's very experience.

He had lost it all - a small fortune - everything. He was at zero.

So again, I ask - when people have zero - what allows some to get it all back and more vs. others that can barely take a step forward and go seemingly nowhere?

The answer to this question is exactly why this book - and the self-help, personal growth category exists - is so vitally important for you and for me.

Here's the answer: It is 1) what they know and 2) what they do.

Confession: I am a self-help book junkie - over the past 40-50 years, I have read and re-read literally hundreds of books within this category. Many of the core concepts of building a successful life appear time and time again: dreams, goals, perseverance, fall down-get up, passion, etc. These recurring themes should be expected, just as books about hiking will include content regarding trails, hiking shoes, backpacks, maps, first aid, and the skills required for a successful expedition.

So, what makes the best books (like this one) stand out in their categories?

The answers to this question are exactly what makes *Run with the Cheetahs* so special. There are 4 big things that make this book stand out in the field:

1. Bring something NEW and FRESH to the reader (JF's "wild kingdom" analogies are new, fresh, and brilliant!)
2. The voice or style of the author (strong, clear, reassuring, and ultimately supportive - you can feel his desire for you to succeed.)
3. The impact of the stories (Stories are most often what a reader takes away from a book, and the stories contained within these pages are compelling and memorable.)
4. The format of the book (immensely beneficial whether read from start to finish or picked up anywhere for instant inspiration)

My relationship with the author spans the best part of 40 years. I have known him as a business associate and friend - but not until now as an author. Am I surprised at how good this book is? No, not at all. Jerry is an extraordinary human being who follows his own advice for success in all his endeavors. In his heart of hearts, he doesn't want to be an author - he wants to be a helper. He wants to help YOU get everything in life that YOU dream of.

Are YOU ready to get started on your climb to an extraordinary life?

Let's GO!

INTRODUCTION

**The best reason for doing the right thing today
…is tomorrow.**

Okay Jerry, who the hell do you think you are to write a book on living an extraordinary life?

You have no credentials to back it up. You don't have a PhD. You're not well-versed in psychology. You struggled academically your whole life. You have failed more times than I can count. You lived through hell more than once, and lost millions of dollars multiple times. Hell, you're not even a good writer!

Yes, that's what you can say about me, and every word is true. And that's exactly why you should engage with me on this journey.

I'm from the real world, just like you, from down in the trenches, deeply experienced and educated from the school of hard knocks. I've done everything the hard way, which I have learned is the only way to climb the ladder of success.

If you lack confidence and are insecure like I was about your capabilities and your future, rest assured, you are not alone. In fact, this is perfectly normal. Almost all of us feel this way along the ascent!

Our tendency to comply, conform, and be mediocre predominately comes from our completely incompetent education system. Dr Jordan Peterson describes it as a system designed in the late 1800s to produce obedient industrial workers, not sovereign citizens. The system saps children of their creativity and ambition. In fact, I was almost dismissed from my elementary school and sent to reform school for my noncompliance with their perceived normalization.

I was what was called a "difficult child." From the first grade, there was no way I would stay in that seat, controlled like a dog in obedience school. The school administration had never faced a challenge like me before. Sitting still in any capacity was just not an option for me. This resulted in spending most of my elementary school years in the principal's office or with various therapists and psychologists.

These people made me repeat second grade, not because of my grades or abilities, but so I would have time to "mature." In reality, I was already the mature one. None of that shit worked. I was born this way and was on a mission to be me, and no authority figure was going to stop me.

After the first month of fifth grade, my teacher refused to let me in the class. She had no patience or any idea how to handle me. The school moved me to a class with a male teacher who they thought would be a better role model. Wrong, again.

My mother was a rock through this period. She defended me every step of the way. She stood her ground when they wanted to drug me. Thank God for her support. Without it, there was no telling where I would have ended up.

There was a big meeting between my parents and the school administration before I entered the 6th grade. They decided they would put me in a class with a firm, tough-as-nails teacher who could "handle me."

On the very first day, I did my usual crap to disrupt class by antagonizing other students, shooting spitballs, making fart noises, and anything else I could do to get kicked out of class. Mrs. Campbell, who was in her sixties, calmly took me out in the hallway.

Without warning, she grabbed me by my shirt, picked me up off the ground, and slammed me up against the wall. My head smacked the wall hard, and she got an inch from my face with her stinky breath and said, "Young man, you are not leaving my class today or any day."

Then she let me down, lowered her voice, and said, "You and I are going to get along just fine. We are going to be best friends."

I was crying at this point, absolutely terrified of her. I had no idea what she meant, but I knew serious authority when I saw it, so I shut up and went back to class.

From that moment forward, my life changed. Mrs. Campbell understood that different kids learn in different ways and that I needed to be extremely challenged, in motion, and kept busy 100% of the time. She made sure that every day, I was challenged with something that interested me, making all of the learning parts of the curriculum like a game. Most importantly, Mrs. Campbell had high expectations for me. She *cared* about me. She was the first person outside my family who made me feel some value for myself.

This resulted in a confidence boost. Sometimes, all anyone needs is an avenue to feel good about themselves. She gave me that path. For all of you teachers like Mrs. Campbell - and I know there are a lot of you out there - your impact on a child's life is immeasurable. Mrs. Campbell saved my life.

"No rules, no laws" is a concept you'll hear from me later in this book. You will also be introduced to the "Ladder of the Cheetah." All that matters in life are *results*! In order to live an extraordinary life you will need to pursue extreme results. Most of the time, those extreme results are not in alignment with the rules and laws dictated by the mass conforming society.

"There is nothing more common than a genius derelict."
--Earl Nightengale

If you're a constant rule-breaker, you are already on your way up the ladder. Who determined that each of us should conform to any universally structured education system? Most rules and laws are designed to control the Sheep produced by our flawed methods of learning. We all learn differently and instinctively. Some of us learn from what we read, some from what we hear, some of us have to watch a process before it sinks in, some of us have to get our hands dirty before anything sticks – and most of us combine one or more different learning styles. But few of us learn at our best sitting in a classroom as we are forced to regurgitate stacks of irrelevant information. What does that experience teach us except how to sit still and accept the boredom of routine? Do you see my point now?

"I never let schooling get in the way of my education."
--Mark Twain

In spite of amazing teachers and coaches who may mentor kids to feel great about themselves, like my life-changing sixth-grade teacher, our education system can be blamed for the brutal attack on self-esteem and self-concept of children. What's being taught in many of our colleges today is a complete travesty. Equality is no longer about accountability. "What part of someone else's earnings are you entitled to?"

We also are in the era of "participation trophies," which imply that no one fails. But failing leads us to the path of success and an ascent up the Ladder of the Cheetah. What are we teaching our youth? A kid who sucks at sports may be a genius musician or engineer, but if he thinks he's a baseball star through false patronizing, he will never find his path to his true greatness. Having a high IQ will not make you stand out; competence, execution, and leadership will.

Who remembers taking a class called "Success 101" in high school? What about an upper-level class in college, "How to Grow and Manage my Assets 401?" Probably none of you; certainly not me. Those aren't things that our schools want kids to know.

Just because you were not a proficient reader, could not comprehend mathematical formulas, or did not have the ability to sit still in class does not make you any less of an intelligent child than anyone else. This is why, later in life, you will see many times the "A" students end up working for the "C" students. If education is your thing, at least get your triple major in common sense, commitment, and work ethic!

Learn to be on the prowl like a Cheetah

The ways of getting results are variable, but there are commonalities that I have learned over a lifetime that I will teach you, allowing you to climb your own ladder to an extraordinary life. There are several topics I will cover in this book that will help you avoid wasting time and hone in on success. You will learn to build an unbreakable foundation within if you are willing to get unreasonable with yourself.

Remember, however, that extraordinary does not mean euphoric. You may envision life in a state of permanent euphoria, but euphoria is a temporary illusion. Crisis in life is a mirror of euphoria. Most importantly, neither endure in the long run!

Our culture will tell you there is some fairytale path in life to happiness, pleasure, elation, and joy. Let's clear this up right from the start. This is a false vision and a losing game to play! Your life will be hard, full of controversy, setbacks, and heartache, but if you play the game properly, it will also yield joy, elation, contentment, and peace of mind. The person you will spend the most time with is *yourself*, so you better like yourself, or you will spend your life with unwelcome company.

As humans, we are all made up of six basic emotions with 27 subset emotions that direct our lives minute to minute. Understanding that the emotional portion of our brains make up a significantly larger part than our logical rational part is the explanation as to why we behave many times in a detrimental manner and have a strong tendency to repeat those negative behaviors. As we move through the content of this book, I will share with you my personal methods used to guide and control the emotional opinion-biased brain.

According to the principles of human nature, if you want to live an extraordinary life you will experience great victories and suffer devastating defeats. It's how we react to both that will determine your ascent up the ladder or your descent down. We will explore this "Ladder of the Cheetah" in detail. It's your climb to an exceptional life or descend into a life of regrets. The choice will be yours!

I have made millions and lost millions multiple times, suffered heartbreak of incomprehensible proportions, and have all the similar weaknesses and insecurities that every one of us possesses. On the other hand, I have had a series of wins that emanated from my losses, which enabled me to continue my climb despite multiple significant setbacks, landing in the extraordinary life I possess today.

At the writing of this book, I am 64 years old. I have been contemplating this book for more than 15 years, and I have finally reached a point where it is my complete obligation to share my story. This book is not something I wanted to do, but it is something I had to do. I will explain what I have learned through my life experiences, self-learning, and observations, despite exposing all of my personal vulnerabilities of the past.

I have studied successful people for more than 30 years and have gained extensive, valuable, and sharable knowledge along the way. Use me as a resource! As you move through the book, you will see many of my learning resources in the form of quotes, stories, and information. Whenever you see a name or author referenced to a quote or story, that is someone you should get aligned with.

My first bit of recommended content comes now! Tim Grover is the legendary trainer of Michael Jordan and Kobe Bryant. No book is aligned more or complements my concepts and theories more than Tim Grovers' *Winning*. This book is the truth spoken in your face! Can you handle it? Whether you read it or listen to it, this content will build your foundation to get the maximum results from *Run with the Cheetahs*.

The Cheetah is the fastest land animal on earth. It has 2,000 unique spots but has no roar! Ready to run with them?
Ready to be one of them? Let's go!

CHAPTER ONE

WELCOME TO THE JUNGLE

"Every morning in Africa, a gazelle wakes up; it knows it must outrun the fastest lion, or it will be killed. Every morning in Africa, a lion wakes up. It knows it must run faster than the slowest gazelle, or it will starve. It doesn't matter whether you're a lion or a gazelle. When the sun comes up, you'd better be running."
--Christopher McDougall

Throughout human civilization there has been a hierarchy. All individuals falling into specific categories. This is not only a natural human process, but also necessary for the very survival of human civilization. This is universal in all social species. Casually, we call it a "pecking order."

In the field of biology, this pecking order is a social ranking system that emerges within animal groups when they interact with one another. Within this hierarchy, there is a dominant individual, often referred to as an alpha, and a submissive individual, known as a beta. The establishment of dominance can occur through various types of interactions, such as displays of aggression or direct physical violence, depending on the species. In social groups, members often compete for limited resources and opportunities to mate. Rather than engaging in constant physical fights, individuals of the same sex establish a relative rank, with higher-ranking individuals typically having greater access to resources and mates. This social order is shaped by repeated interactions and can change whenever a subordinate individual challenges a dominant one.

Let's take a look at how this works in modern society, I will describe the different types of social humans that exist today. First, ask yourself: where am I in the pecking order? Is this where I want to be? Am I willing to go to battle to climb up the pecking order?

Humans are the most dangerous animals. We have killed more of our own kind than any other animal on earth. Understand what we are capable of, and the ancient savagery within us. Other animals kill through instinct. Humans kill through instinct and knowledge. We are a dangerous species, and you need to have your defenses up at all times.

With that said, when it comes to your personal human nature in the modern world, you want to harness your danger and remain in control of your capabilities but have the ability to unleash your fury when required.

The best way to describe the different levels of human execution is to relate to animal behavior. This way you can get a clear metaphoric understanding by the way various humans behave and their related outcomes in the Jungle called life.

SNAKES – The Deceitful 5% (intentionally untrustworthy)

As in the animal kingdom, Snakes come in different guises and sizes. Some Snakes will kill with a single bite; others may just terrify us as they slither around. Some Snakes are beautiful...until they strike! The same applies to the "Snakes" in the human population.

The world is full of Snakes, and they will devour you at any chance they get, without remorse or pity. The main difference between Snakes and the other personality types is *intention*. Anyone can make a mistake or have a misfortune, but Snakes make the same mistakes and the same choices repeatedly. Moreover, a Snake sets out with bad intentions or resorts to bad intentions when things do not go their way. Snakes have an evil streak inside them that allows them to be consciously cruel with little remorse or feeling. It's generally a narcissistic trait that was developed through life's experiences as a child.

Do not try to rescue a Snake; it is impossible. They cannot be fixed. The Snake has an evil streak and ice within their soul that allows for unconscionable behavior. Do not give them a second chance or future opportunities to be part of your life in any manner. A Snake will repeatedly shed his skin and reappear as an imposter. Snakes should be avoided at all costs. They are poisonous to success. Snakes are not only detrimental to your financial well-being; they can come in the form of vindictiveness, revenge, and bad emotional intent. Any type of relationship with a Snake has no future, especially in personal relationships.

Run, run, run.

Unfortunately, from my perspective, Snakes have become a higher percentage of the population over the past 20 years. There are many reasons for this. Cheating is easier through technology, as the web creates a worldwide market for the Snakes. There, we find fewer guidelines to hold lawless individuals accountable. The ever-widening wealth gap makes people feel left behind and entitled to things unearned. The worldwide web gives a platform for the most vicious Snakes to execute their evil, including child sex slavery and elaborate devastating scam operations.

I have dealt with multiple kinds of Snakes in my life. Being receptive to a Snake attack has a lot to do with your confidence, ethics, intuition, and self-esteem. The weak and uneducated are easily manipulated. During the first half of my life, I fell into that category. I was a victim of poor relationships, conflict, and scams.

In fact, I even lost over a million dollars to a complex Ponzi scheme. I now realize that I made myself accessible to these situations through my inability to trust myself. The good news is that in the second half of my life, I turned the tide to live an exemplary life by sniffing out the Snakes and running for the hills if one gets near me.

Even with this knowledge, I've still had a few run ins with some highly sophisticated Snakes. Remember, they are everywhere and it's impossible to completely escape them. No matter how careful, diligent, or smart you are, Snakes are just as smart and they will infiltrate and attack at every opportunity.

Of course, you will learn in this book how to minimize your exposure and then how to react when a Snake bites you. But be prepared, they are coming for you! They are drawn to success, so they can suck off of it like parasites, or even steal it from you if they can. Snakes have existed since the beginning of time and will always exist as they are part of the hierarchy.

Our world is designed to control Snakes through laws and natural consequences that will inevitably happen to Snakes in the long run. Remember that "No one gets away with anything…eventually!" This means that being a Snake is a losing game 100% of the time. Whenever you reach any level of apparent achievement or success through unethical or manipulative ways, it will not last. Furthermore, as you read further into this book, you will realize that your inner moral core is a key component to achieving the ultimate goal of serenity in your life. Being a Snake in any form relinquishes the opportunity to become a person of inner peace and serenity.

SLOTHS – The Victim 5% (It's someone else's fault, it's someone else's problem)

Sloths spend much of their lives in the canopy, snoozing and remaining hidden from predators. The animal lives a solitary, sedentary life. They sit high above the world alone, sluggish, and sleeping most of the day.

In some respects, the Sloths are a sadder story than the Snakes. These are people with no goals, no dreams, no drive, no vision, and no determination. Furthermore, they take zero accountability for anything and blame their circumstances on outside sources. They decide that they are victims of the world and their surroundings, and the odds of them ever escaping this mindset are extremely low. Everything about them is "someone else's" issue to resolve. Sloths not only have poor self-esteem, but they are also generally not healthy human beings. I have found that individuals with this deep victim mentality will spill their negativity to anyone and everything they come into contact with. You cannot save a Sloth, and a Sloth will never be an asset to you, so avoiding them is best.

SHEEP – The Conformist 89% (Go along to get along)

The vast majority of humans are Sheep. The Sheep is a risk-averse conformer. They seek mediocrity. They comply with the status quo and feel safe with the herd. Sheep have dreams that stay dreams and rarely take actions necessary to propel them up the next rung of the ladder.

A Sheep is vulnerable to the complacency that society portrays as a normal life. They live an average life, and thrive on balance. The work and drive to be exceptional at anything is simply too overwhelming for a Sheep. They accept their plight in life due to vast insecurities and spend their life looking for the path of least resistance.

There is nothing ethically wrong with being a Sheep. Sheep can be polite, trustworthy, loving, caring human beings. However, as years roll by, Sheep succumb to the death knell of life: regret. Sheep, in their later years, eventually say, "I would have, should have, could have…I wish I had…If only…" as they review their lives.

The biggest regrets of old age are the things we didn't do. Sheep wish they had spent time pursuing more of their goals, dreams and visions. If after reading this book you decide to be content being a Sheep I want you to be the best possible Sheep you can be and at least be the head of the herd. However, always remember that the first-place Sheep is miles behind the last place Cheetah.

CHEETAHS – The Climber 1% (Execution, Vision, Action)

The Cheetah is on the chase, moves quickly, and is a hunter. Action and execution come in front of detailed analysis. The Cheetah learns as it grows and may be victim to many mistakes and setbacks along the way, but the climb is a relentless one. Cheetahs are visionaries that see the dream and create the goals and related actions to get there. They are nimble, take risks, adapt, and can change course in the blink of an eye. They run so fast that obstacles are a blur. Their work ethic is unshakeable. They make quick decisions and understand that the wrong ones can be fixed later. The Cheetah takes accountability for everything and thrives on responsibility. Cheetahs eat Sheep for a snack.

Unlike a Snake, Sloth, or Sheep, who are likely to remain mostly stagnant their entire lives, the Cheetah is aggressively active for decades. These are the learning and growing years where knowledge and experience are gained in mass. Cheetahs are rare. They only represent 1% of the hierarchy of humans. When you hear about the "1%" discussed about anything related to successful people, these are the Cheetahs. Although the Snakes, Sloths, and Sheep rarely become Cheetahs, Cheetahs do evolve to become Falcons or Lions. The faster they run and compress time in the learning process, the quicker a Falcon or Lion may be born.

"The Arena" – The Cheetah's Mantra

"It is not the critic who counts; not the man who points out how the strong man stumbles or where the doer of deeds could have done them better. The credit belongs to the man who is actually in the arena, whose face is marred by dust and sweat and blood; who strives valiantly; who errs, who comes short again and again, because there is no effort without error and shortcoming; but who

does actually strive to do the deeds; who knows great enthusiasms, the great devotions; who spends himself in a worthy cause; who at the best knows in the end the triumph of high achievement, and who at the worst, if he fails, at least fails while daring greatly, so that his place shall never be with those cold and timid souls who neither know victory nor defeat."

—Theodore Roosevelt

FALCONS -The Analyst 1/10 0f 1 % (Focus on the details)

The Falcon is a rare breed. He soars above the crowd with ease and grace but can also accelerate in an instant to 240 mph, the fastest animal on Earth, leaving everyone and everything in his wake. The Falcon is a refined, seasoned Cheetah. He's been in the trenches and emerged smarter and more sophisticated. Not everyone can be a Falcon! Falcons evolve from Cheetahs. The Cheetah goes from being on the prowl to hunting his prey in a smarter way.

What separates the Cheetah from the Falcon is that the Falcon has learned to focus on details and efficiencies, not just the effort or work ethic. The Falcon is a seasoned, calculating professional who gets his strategic advantage through detailed thought and calm, consistent execution. The Falcon uses his talent and experience to see the playing field differently than others. He understands the psychology of how people think and act and uses that knowledge to leverage himself through leadership skills and loyal relationships.

ALPHA LIONS – The Elite 1/1000 of 1% (Innovation)

The Alpha Lion is the rarest of species, reached only by the most elite individuals. He or she cannot be caged and can break through anything. The main thing that separates Alpha Lions from Falcons and Cheetahs is innovation. They operate at a higher intelligence level than the rest of us and use their intelligence to conquer all. The Alpha Lion is a revolutionary who achieves the impossible and brings the world along with them.

Just a few examples are Steve Jobs, Margaret Thatcher, Martin Luther King, Tiger Woods, Wayne Gretsky, Abraham Lincoln, Elon Musk, Simone Biles, Jeff Bezos, Thomas Edison, Oprah Winfrey, Albert Einstein, Tom Brady, Muhammad Ali or Michael Jordan. All these revolutionaries redefined their areas of expertise through innovation. They achieved what seemed impossible.

However, they have little life balance. They are laser-focused on the target and are always 100% confident in the process to get there. Be careful if you meet an Alpha Lion. Alpha Lions are calm, kind, and avoid conflict, but the storm can be seconds away. Their tolerance for victimization and conformity is zero. You either perform to their standards, or you will be gone. The Alpha Lion doesn't compete – he dominates, requires 100% loyalty, and will chew you up and spit you out. Unlike all of the other Jungle animals, the Alpha Lion has some genetic components that make him a unique human being. Let us just say that they are gifted.

Tim Grover, in his book *Relentless,* calls the Alpha Lions "Cleaners." A Cleaner has the guts and the vision to steer everything to their advantage. You never know what they're going to do, but you know something's coming, and all you can do is wait and watch, with fear and respect for their ability to handle anything without discussion or analysis. These are the most driven individuals you will ever know, with an unmatched genius for what they do: they don't just perform a job; they reinvent it.

Moving up the Ladder of the Cheetah

Many of you reading this book might be Sheep, and you are reading it because you sense something is missing from your life. You know there is more out there! This thought process alone is a launching pad for your climb. In later chapters, you will see how the Ladder of the Cheetah can get you out of complacency. You will be on the path to becoming a Cheetah, which is my desire for you, because once you are a Cheetah, regret becomes a thing of the past, and the eventuality of an extraordinary life moves within your reach.

"When the flood comes, you want to be the person who built the ark."
--Dr Jordan Peterson

CHAPTER TWO

THE LADDER FOUNDATION

"There is no elevator to success...you must take the stairs."
--Zig Ziglar

I spent 11 years of my life in the golf world, from ages 12 to 23. I played Division 1 college golf on a full-ride scholarship and achieved a varsity letter 2 of my 4 years. Playing at this level enabled me to gain association with many elite players of the game, both amateur and professional. During my senior year, I also had an opportunity to caddy on the PGA tour, where I was introduced to the best of the best. I even got to chat with Jack Nicklaus on the driving range.

The beauty of the game of golf is that compared to all other sports, the lessons learned are the same lessons required to live a successful, extraordinary life. The key factor is that it pits you against yourself. There are no teammates, no referees, no judges, and 100% self-accountability for the rules and ethics of the game. Just you and the playing field, which in this case is the golf course, your mindset, and the conditions presented on any given day.

Many consider golf to be the most difficult sport to excel at. There is no such thing as a naturally great golfer, as you hear in other sports. "He/she is such a great natural athlete," or they can be gifted genetically as well. Did you know that only .05% of golfers will ever shoot a round under par, and only about 1 % will ever carry a scratch handicap, which means that they average shooting around par?

So here we go again with the analogy that applies to all high-level successes: It's the 1%!

This brings me to the concept that is so misunderstood about living a lifelong extraordinary life. It's just as difficult and hard as achieving the 1% in any given area of excellence. To climb the rungs on the ladder like a Cheetah, you must start with a solid foundation for your ladder to stand on. If your efforts in life are based on a shaky foundation, it's not likely to stand up over time. It is imperative that you lay the foundation firmly. So, let's take a look at how you can start shooting par in the game of life.

Always remember, no one is coming to the rescue!

"If it is to be, it is up to me."
--William Johnsen

Persistence: Focus on your short-term mindset – What I am doing right now – Developing the subconscious minds positive flow.

Accountability: Engage in and speak the truth 100% of the time – Stop lying to yourself. Be accountable for everything in your control and out of your control.

Reliability: On time all the time – Count on yourself – Be the go-to person

Responsibility: Ingrain obsessive positive habits. It's on me!

Resilience: Learn to adapt, pivot, and redirect but never quit .

In order to gain the characteristics of a highly extraordinary life, these 5 foundations of behavior are essential. They will affect your relationships, loyalty, career, health, and financial well-being. It is imperative to start climbing your ladder rung by rung as soon as possible in life, and in order to do that, you must be committed and grounded in shooting **PARRR** in life.

With that said, there is one missing component to the theory above. Without it, this is just another book spewing content that might be implemented in theory but will be forgotten in a week or two. All 5 structures of the foundation will require the one most important action that is shared by all elite individuals. In fact, without it, you are simply wasting your time.

Discipline: In fact, discipline is so important that it is the essential principle one of the 5 foundations that turns your life of shooting **PARRR** to a lifelong **PARRR-D.** I'm not talking about a party that you attend or a party with music, dancing, drinking, and/or whatever else you prefer at a party. This is your internal party. It's your self-esteem, your inner moral core, and how you feel about yourself. Unlike a party you may attend for a few hours, this **PARRR-D** lasts a lifetime. Consider it the greatest drug ever invented.

> "The best way to predict the future is to create it."
> – Abraham Lincoln

CHAPTER THREE

THE DREAM STEALERS

"You are the only you there ever was,
and you are the only you there will ever be."
--Denis Waitley

Each of us is a human animal made up of 4 trillion cells, yet each one of us is unique. Nobody has ever lived the same set of experiences as you. While your core beliefs and values remain consistent, who you are changes slightly from moment to moment based on the experiences you have and your thoughts about them. You are the result of a complete, unrepeatable series of events from the moment you are born – and remember, you are a major part of that series of events. The world doesn't just happen to you. You happen to the world.

Being the miracle that we are, have you ever wondered why we engage in self-destructive behaviors both mentally and physically?

From a logical standpoint, it makes no sense whatsoever that we, as humans, have the ability to destroy ourselves.

However, from an emotional standpoint, it's not really a surprise. We exist operating from our emotional impulses. This is why controlling your emotions and understanding the game of life is essential to making yourself the best version of you.

Dream stealers come in the form of four categories, all of which will quickly sap you of your determination, hopes, goals and dreams. In fact, dealing with the dream stealers is inevitable, so facing your demons head on right now is a requirement for evolving into a Cheetah. Use the information in this chapter to put your excuses in the grave forever.

Some of these are common Sheep behaviors that paralyze you into your conforming ways. You are an addict to your lifestyle. These detrimental behaviors are sure to slowly, year by year, send you on a decent down your ladder. Remember, if you want your situation to change, you need to change. Consider this your "awareness chapter." The steps to reverse your climb and start heading up the Ladder of the Cheetah will be presented in later chapters.

Four categories of dream stealers

Drugs/Alcohol. First, man takes a drink…then the drink takes the man!
Self-medicating techniques equal one thing: trouble. Anything from wasted time and money to outright ruin or even death. Drugs and alcohol cause damage to internal organs. They kill brain cells – intoxication is quite literally your brain being starved of oxygen. You can justify your casual use in any way you want, but people who live extraordinary lives do not engage in destructive behaviors, not even a little bit! Whenever you escape to anything that's externally mind-altering, it becomes the subliminal focus of your life.

The Sheep have two glasses of wine with dinner. Even if you are a casual drinker or marijuana smoker, you look forward to that escape after work or on the weekends. When a negative escape becomes your dominant thought, it, in turn, becomes impossible to positively affect your subconscious mind. In fact, you are reenforcing the negative, which we will discuss at length later. The Cheetahs, Falcons, and Lions don't need to wind down at the end of the day. They look for ways to wind up 24/7 in obsessive behaviors and then carefully plan their escape time. If you have any type of drug, alcohol, gambling, sex, or food addiction, I suggest you seek professional help immediately!

Poor habits. Your daily habits have more to do with outcomes in your life and impact your destiny more than any other influence. How you behave daily related to every aspect of your existence will determine your climb or your fall. Everything is on the table here. We do not want to be average at anything, so eliminating detrimental habits will be a big part of your battle. We are shooting for exceptional. *Change Your Habits, Change Your Life* by Tom Corley, is a great place to start understanding of the impact of your daily habits and the process of changing them.

Negative people/bad relationships. Toxicity in your relationships is a slow drain on your mental and physical resources that will decay your very being over time. We must avoid the Snakes altogether and stop feeling sorry for or enabling the Sloths. Eliminating negative people and any type of bad influence is a non-negotiable on the way to an extraordinary life. Many times, toxic people can be family members, close friends, or work relationships. Regardless of the source, they must go. This is one of the hardest concepts to understand and implement. We are only going to associate with those who are going to climb our ladder with us and support us through the setbacks. Only allies are allowed! You need to become bullet-proof of anyone stealing your dreams. Also, when people write you off, don't write back!

Yourself. You might be your own worst dream stealer! Becoming a victim of past events and whatever detriments have occurred in your life is the biggest dream-stealer of them all. It's paralyzing and will cause a slow descent down your ladder. Who do you believe you are? How do you see and feel about yourself? What is the impact of low self-esteem? We will look at this destructive mindset more carefully in the chapter "Victor or Victim?"

*"When a person can't find a deep sense of meaning,
they distract themselves with pleasure."*
--Victor Frankel

Are you buying painkillers or vitamins? We all want the painkillers, but the healing is in the vitamins. Your mind is an incredibly powerful, sophisticated computer. Every time you treat it badly, you infect it with a virus, and eventually, it will not operate efficiently. Some of you will need a virus scan, removal, and a reboot, but either way, if you want a high-performing brain to lead you to an extraordinary life, you need to clean your hard drive and keep it that way.

Detrimental habits

The reason we are so ready to engage in bad behaviors is because we crave instant gratification, and most of the time, the effects don't show up for a while. "It won't kill me now!" we think. We prefer the "Devil We Know" to the unknown, so we're willing to stay in toxic relationships and engage in detrimental habits rather than run the risk of being alone. We like the comfort of blaming others for our problems. What's good *to* you is not always good *for* you.

But detrimental obsessive behaviors will kill us sooner than we would have died otherwise – and in some cases, *much* sooner.

"I know a guy who smoked two packs a day and lived to be 90," we hear people say. Yet without smoking, he might have made it to 100. You also need to ask about this individual's quality of life. Would he have felt better with less illness, fewer health issues, and more energy? Would he have smelled better to his friends and family? Would he have done something amazing with the money he *wasn't* spending on cigarettes? Just because a smoker lives to be 90 doesn't mean smoking didn't damage them in a thousand other ways. Life is a game of odds and percentages. The example above certainly does not put the odds in your favor.

As we age, we tend to create bad habits that are counter to our best interests. As special and unique as we are, why would we ever think about doing something that harms what you've been given? Why would you ever wish to diminish the miracle of your existence? Give up things that are not projecting you up your ladder!

It's a natural human instinct to "escape." We all have our pressures and insecurities. Things from our pasts bother us. Many people use those excuses, consciously or subconsciously, to engage in escapism behaviors that create extremely unhealthy habits: drugs, alcohol, poor health, bad relationships, and diet habits. I believe it all comes from the need to escape who you are as well as your stubborn belief in the lies you tell yourself about yourself.

Escape in itself is not bad. We all need a break; we all need to step away, but how we do this can determine your ascent up the ladder or your demise down the ladder. The trick is to escape to things that are Cheetah-like behaviors, and good for us, which will keep our vision moving forward.

We should escape into regimented, obsessive, positive behaviors. Everybody has to escape; there is nobody who just lives in neutral, feeling okay all the time. Eventually, we need to mentally escape reality one way or another. All Cheetahs escape into something positive. The trick is that they plan their escape time and then get right back to the battle.

We must ask ourselves what we are willing to give up or eliminate. What you choose to walk away from can be more important than what you walk towards. Stop looking for happiness in the same place you lost it. Use your weekends to build the life you want, not to escape the life you have.

I prefer health and fitness as a habit; that's the easiest escape. It's easy to measure and track, and we enjoy an immediate feeling from it due to a dopamine release in our brain that's actually good for us. Tap into the drug! I do every day. Related areas would include meditation, yoga, or any type of mindfulness. People who escape into other positive behaviors, like studying or practicing a skill, also have the right idea, but results may take longer to show up.

Diet and nutrition can be another excellent way to escape. Set up a challenge to feel as good as you can feel each day when you awaken. Escape alone on a hike or a day away to celebrate yourself. I urge you to experience what I call extreme health, where through regimented exercise and proper nutrition, your mind and body perform at an exceptional level. Are you running like a 10-year-old car with 100k miles on it or performing like a 610-horsepower Lamborghini Huracan? Until you experience this feeling, you will never know the quality of life you can live. I call extreme health the greatest drug ever! Oh, and by the way, it doesn't wear off after an hour or two. Instead of a hangover, you will have a flyover. You will feel ecstatic 24/7. With every win, even the minor victories, there is a small dopamine hit.

Addictive behaviors can create a marathon runner or a heroine junkie; the result depends on specific chosen behaviors.

Obsessive positive behaviors

I once heard, "*Obsession is a gift, not a disease.*"

I hear and see all the time parents complaining about their child being obsessed with something. "All he wants to do is practice baseball. Every day after school until the sun goes down!" "She dances all day and night." They may see an obsession and discourage it. But when I see a kid obsessed with something, I know it's a kid on their way to success. It's certainly better than the kid coming home to eat junk food, watch TV, or play violent video games all evening. I saw an interview with Mark Cuban where he stated, "Pursue what you're good at, not your passion."

I would highly encourage young people to find what they are good at and pursue it. If you're good at something and pursue it, nothing will build your self-esteem faster than a natural ability to do something well. At the end of the day, building confidence and feeling good about yourself is the secret sauce to resilience when climbing your ladder and avoiding the Dream Stealers.

I can love basketball all I want, and have a deep passion for it – but I'm 5'9" with a one-foot vertical leap and short arms. Am I ever going to be a great basketball player? Probably not. Be realistic about passions and remember to pursue your talents. When you pursue talent and combine it with great work ethic, you are in Cheetah mode. Leave your passions for your hobbies unless your passion happens to be something you're great at.

To reiterate, spend time on what you're good at, because young people's self-esteem will be built through the successes they build from doing that. When you have self-esteem and success, you seriously reduce the chances of taking the easy route to the dream stealers down the avenue of intoxication, poor habits, negative people and your own personal demons. Even though you may be good at something, you're putting in the work ethic to get even better at it. You're enjoying that process, which will teach you how to take the hard route. Furthermore, you will naturally seek out the next level as you excel. It is another critical characteristic of the upward climbers. A really good talent finds its happiness in execution.

Personally, I have seen both sides of the fence multiple times. I have engaged in both detrimental habits and positive obsessive behaviors that each took my path in opposite directions. I have had periods in my life where alcohol, drugs, and sex ruled the day. I have also gone to the positive side by engaging in extreme health, building businesses and an amazing marriage. All of us will tend down both paths from time to time, but if you recognize the negative obsessive behaviors early, they can be redirected down the right path.

How many people try to tell us we should have balance in our lives? We hear this all the time, but you won't hear it from me. Nobody achieved anything great by having balance in their life. If you want to be elite at anything or feel exceptional about yourself, obsession will rule the day, and you will not have that balance, at least for an extended period of time. There are times when you simply must go "all in" on what you want to achieve if you intend to be a Cheetah and prowl up your ladder.

My dream stealers, and how I overcame them

Incompatible goals are dream-stealers. I dreamed of playing on the PGA Tour from the time I was fifteen years old. At the same time, however, I engaged in behaviors counter to those dreams. Those were incompatible goals.

I partied all night, chasing girls and having a good time, and that chipped away at my skill, concentration, and potential. I didn't know any better. I didn't have the proper mentor or education. I can't say for sure that if I'd had a good mentor, I would have avoided those behaviors, but avoiding them is what separates a success from a failure. When you see someone in their teens and early 20s who is mature beyond their years, who is obsessively focused on one thing, you know that they are heading for success. They figured out a way to avoid the party years!

From the age of 15-23, and while playing golf for the University of Maryland, I was fully engaged in the party lifestyle, even while wanting to be a professional golfer. One goal simply could not compete with the other, and the goal of partying provided me with instant gratification. Golf was hard. It took work, discipline, and practice. I thought I was working hard at it, and that I was "all in," but I wasn't even close to that. After major back surgery at the age of 22, I slipped into the victimized lifestyle. I gave up on my dreams, and the party lifestyle became the flavor of the day. Eventually, I quit golf.

As time passed, I moved on, married, and had a family. However, my entire existence before my divorce was about living a **reliant life rather than a reliable life.** I was outer-directed and tried to achieve all my success through other people. I latched onto people, thinking they could lead me down a golden path. It wasn't until after my divorce that I was forced to take 100% accountability for myself. In the second half of my life, I am living the opposite: I lead the way, and other people come with me. It's a dream-stealer because, for the first half of my life, I was insecure despite my successes. The outer me appeared to be thriving, while the inner me was an insecure child. I never felt worthy of any success because I always counted on someone else to get me there. When you do it yourself, it's an entirely different feeling! The faster you can overcome your doubts and fears about who you are, the better your life will be. More on this in the chapter "Victor or Victim?

How can a young person defend against the dream stealers?

The reason that few people manage to overcome self-doubt is because they don't know what a problem it is! There is a complete lack of awareness. We just walk around wondering, "Why do I feel this way?"

I hope that this book can help you discover if this is your truth.

Many times, we blame our parents, though their intentions might have been good. Overprotective parents fill us with fear and turn us into weak adults. I was a great athlete as a kid, but I got hurt a lot, and my parents began to keep me out of sports. They were doing what they felt was right, so I don't blame them. But I do think children must learn lessons through experience.

Naturally, we can't let our children do unwarranted, reckless, risky things. But holding them back from what they're good at will make them feel insecure. I feel if I had been able to pursue more sports as a kid and spend more time on things I was good at, I would have felt better about myself. I would have engaged in more personal success.

Unfortunately, in today's world, most of us are raised to be "soft." Children are kept safe from tough times and experiences where they learn from trial and error.

One way to explain this is to take a look at the two dogs in my life. My current dog is a Labradoodle named Benny, and he's the biggest wimp in the world. He's been ours since he was a puppy. Benny is as loving and caring a family pet as you could ever want, but he's confined to the yard, doesn't really do much, and had little exposure to other dogs or the outside world. He's coddled and protected. He's soft!

In contrast, when I was a child, around 7 years old, there was a puppy living at the house behind us. By all standards, he was abused, ignored, and left outside on bitter cold winter nights until one day, when he got old enough to climb over the fence, he showed up at our back door, skinny from malnutrition with blood on his belly from climbing the fence and totally desperate. My parents gave him a blanket and some food and let him sleep on our back porch. My dad called the owner, who told us to take the dog to the pound - so we kept him. This was one of the greatest days of my life. He was a mixed mutt with golden hair, so we named him Nugget.

Back in those days, the dogs in our neighborhood ran around wild and engaged in risky behaviors. Our dog would disappear for an entire day, and sometimes, packs of dogs would roam around and hang out, and they became street-smart. They were allowed to be in an atmosphere that was a little bit dangerous. In turn, Nugget was wise, street-smart, and loyal to the family. He had multiple other dog allies who had each other's backs. He was able to reach his complete potential ability to enjoy being a dog through his experiences and knowledge. Nugget was fully engaged in Cheetah behaviors. In today's world, we don't let our dogs – much less our children – out of our sight. To run like a Cheetah, to ascend your ladder quickly and sustainably, you need to choose right now to be a Nugget, not a Benny!

Responsibility is what leads to quality self-esteem and long-term joy in life for both men and women. If you never take on responsibility, never have anything you must wake up for, achieve, or do, you essentially become a deteriorating sponge. You have no substance.

We want to protect everyone from everything, though historically, according to human nature, we are not made that way. It creates a negative mental view of yourself. **The more responsibility and accountability you can endure, the greater self-concept and life you will live.**

"Even if you're on the right track,
you'll get run over if you just sit there."
--Will Rogers

CHAPTER FOUR

THE GREAT OBSERVER

Everything of value I have ever learned was from watching and listening to other people.

Observation is the process of actively watching to gain more knowledge about our circumstances, and the first thing I recommend is that you become an expert observer.

When I was younger, because of my problems in school, I always considered myself less intelligent than other people. I lacked confidence and was fearful of how I was viewed, especially when communicating. Being called on in class was terrifying. The education system was not designed in a way to teach me anything. However, finding things or people I admired was easy. I then watched them and imitated what I saw.

This advice might sound simplistic, but it's power to launch you to levels of success you never dreamed about will become evident as you move through these chapters. There is a world of difference between "seeing" and "observing." Observing creates curiosity…curiosity leads to creativity… and creativity leads to action and innovation.

My parents ran a souvenir stand at the Washington Senators games. When we were little kids, we used to go with them to summertime games. At ten years old, I sold things at the stand - my very first sales job. I observed vendors out in the stands, selling their own products, so one day, I came in, grabbed the stack of programs, and went into the stands to sell them for 25 cents each. I was fascinated with this new avenue for making a profit. But I wasn't getting paid; this was a family business!

So, back in those days, beer was sold only in glass bottles. There were no cans yet. There were 24 bottles in a case, so cases were quite heavy. The game's beer sellers took one case at a time into the stands. Once that case was sold, they had to get in line to get their next case of beer from the refrigerated truck. That took time and cut into their sales. Well, next to my family's souvenir stand, a group of four men had found a way to speed things up. They came early and set up a cart of about sixty cases of beer with huge bags of ice on top. When they finished selling a case, they didn't have to get back in line with the others; they could just grab the next case off their cart. More sales for them!

The only problem was, the cart sat out in the open, so only three of them at a time could go and sell beer. Someone had to stay behind and watch the merchandise. I observed this process game after game until one day I had an idea that could help them.

They were always friendly with my family because we ran the shop right next door. One day, I just said, "Hey, guys, why don't you let me watch the beer for you? That way, all four of you can go sell." I sat atop this huge pile of beer and ice where I could watch the game, and they paid me a couple bucks every game. They loved having me there. Unfortunately, my dad lost one of his unpaid employees!

Observation gets the wins

What's the difference between someone who practices active observation and someone who doesn't? Plenty. An active observer is constantly asking how or why. It's not just seeing; it's questioning. The difference is what I call active thinking versus passive thinking. Have you ever been driving through a city and thought to yourself, *Who owns these buildings?* or *Who runs these businesses?* Your first question from observing should be based in curiosity: *How can I have one*? All success starts with a vision from some level of observation. The benefits of good observation are varied and powerful. Let's examine how active awareness of your surroundings and circumstances can change your life.

Improve efficiency, accuracy, and attention to detail

Good observers see the gaps in a system and can deduce how to fill them. Observational skills promote attention to detail, ensuring thoroughness.

Make better decisions and use critical thinking

The more we observe, the more information we have, the better our decisions will be. Being observant lets you recognize significant changes or trends early on, enabling you to adapt and respond effectively. We can identify potential challenges or opportunities by paying attention to our surroundings, adjusting our approach, and making informed decisions.

Observation and critical thinking are closely intertwined. For example, observing customer behavior and feedback in a business setting can help identify patterns in purchasing preferences or satisfaction levels. Recognizing these patterns leads to informed decisions regarding product development, marketing strategies, or customer service improvements.

Get roadmaps for problem-solving and achieving goals

If we pay careful attention to those who are successful in doing what we want, we have a path before us. I'm afraid that we often make life ten times harder than necessary! It's just not as difficult as it seems. By stepping back and observing the people doing the things we dream about doing or being, and being open to their experience, will elevate us more quickly than anything else.

Something I distinctly remember from childhood was my strong respect for older people. That seems atypical for most kids. Older people are unfortunately treated as "out of touch" at best, and certainly as if they have nothing valuable to contribute. I was never like that; their experience and knowledge were priceless. I was remarkably close to my grandfather, for example. I had a great uncle who ran a highly successful business. I remember always being drawn to those people and watching what they were doing. We'll discuss this further in the next chapter, "In the Trenches," concerning seeking advice. For now, just remember that observing what success looks like is a terrific teacher.

Becoming a great observer

I have been an observer my entire life. From an early age, I learned the benefits of paying attention to my surroundings and my elders (well – except maybe in school itself!). Observation got me curious and looking into the things that I wanted.

I don't remember my parents specifically teaching me this – I learned by their example rather than by a set of spoken rules - but respect for my elders and for authority figures was an automatic thing for me. I was a polite kid. Therefore, those people were receptive to me and didn't mind having me around. I was able to stay close by and absorb what I could see.

I always wanted money as a kid. My parents were hard workers who always found a way to provide for the family, but we certainly didn't have a lot of disposable income. It wasn't the type of thing where I could ask my dad for a few dollars. I knew not to ask because he didn't have it. This made me restless; I wanted to do things that kids love – arcade games, pinball machines, bowling, and all the other things that a weekly allowance just can't cover. I innovated ways to make money. I had a knack for seeing where money could be made, even by someone as young as I was.

One of the first things I remember doing happened when I was nine. My mother took us grocery shopping at a large local supermarket. At the time, there were no attendants or clerks who would help people take their groceries to their cars. My brothers and I were the ones who loaded the car. In observing this, I thought, "Hey, if I rode my bike up here, I could help people load their cars, and I might make a little money doing that." I started loading bags into cars for people, and they paid me. A quarter here, 50 cents there. I'd take my tips and play pinball at the bowling alley. The next day, I'd go back and do it all again.

Early on in my life, getting the things I wanted motivated me to look for gaps to fill, for ways to make myself useful. I figured out early in life that in order to get the things I wanted, it was going to be up to me to make that happen. I watched my elders; I learned from their experiences. I drove myself to succeed out of sheer rebellion against those who might think I was less intelligent or capable than my peers.

However, this doesn't mean I haven't made mistakes or that I can't become even more observant. Nor does it mean that those who have never been particularly observant can't improve. Here are some steps we can take to improve our powers of observation.

Be present

One of the fundamental aspects of observation is being fully present in the moment. Get off your device and pay attention to your surroundings. Practice mindfulness by consciously focusing on your surroundings without getting distracted by other thoughts or stimuli. Take a moment to pause and take in the details of your environment, using your senses to gather information. By training your mind to be present, you can sharpen your observation skills and notice details that may have previously gone unnoticed.

Engage in new activities and learning

Expanding your experiences and knowledge base can significantly enhance your observation skills. Engage in new activities, explore different environments, and learn about diverse subjects. By exposing yourself to unfamiliar situations, you train your mind to be more observant and adaptable.

I'm a big believer in questions. If we are willing to embrace our curiosity and ask questions of smart people about things we don't understand, we engage in the same type of learning.

I was on a flight where, for some reason, I was seated separately from my family. Instead, I was next to a boy of about eleven, and his parents were also seated elsewhere. So he and I had a long conversation – which *he* started. He introduced himself and asked me what I did. At that age, that kind of curiosity and imitativeness is unusual. He conducted himself in a manner where he could easily carry on a conversation with an adult. This young man had a solid foundation, and he'd been taught how to have a conversation with someone older than himself. On that flight, he probably asked me twenty questions, and he told me all about himself. Clearly, I had met a fellow observer!

Conclusion

Everything of value I have ever learned was from watching and listening to other people. Taking this one step further, every great thing that has ever happened in my life evolved from some level of observation that led me to beneficial relationships. Developing and honing our observation skills enhances our understanding of the world and enriches our personal and professional interactions. By embracing the power of observation, we actively participate in the now, increasing our opportunities and fostering growth, empathy, and positive change. This crucial skill will be a facet of every bit of advice I give.

If you look carefully, the world is rigged in your favor!

CHAPTER FIVE

IN THE TRENCHES

"I'll be your coach, but I will not be your friend."
- Herb Brooks
USA Hockey Olympic Coach of 1983 Miracle Team

Always listen twice…
first to what's being said, then to who said it.

No one ever accused me of being a nice guy. Good-hearted, kind, loyal, committed, yes. But nice? Not really. Seeking "nice" people is rolling the dice. Most of us are naturally attracted to superficially nice people. That person that's the life of the party, you know, the fun one.

Well, take a look when the party's over. If only you could see behind closed doors! You will discover that the most successful people are people who do not patronize but stand their ground and speak the truth. Their foundation, principles, and inner core are on a solid footing. They will not violate their values to appease people or operate in a politically correct mode.

If you run into a tough, hardnosed personality when seeking advice do not take it personally. They will not likely become your friend, but they may become your ally.

I used to coach youth hockey. I had only played hockey casually as a kid; I didn't know the game in detail. But when my kids started the game, I began reading and learning and became an assistant coach at our local club. There just weren't that many coaches in our area for hockey, and since I was always successful as a coach in other sports, I thought I'd jump in. I had a good history of getting kids to feel good about themselves through work ethic and improved performance. My track record in coaching with baseball and hockey was quite good. Next thing I knew, I was coaching a travel league, a fairly high-level of competitive hockey for young players.

After five years of coaching, doing a lot of reading and trying to improve my knowledge of the game, a gentleman named Gordy Lane was helping out with coaching at the highest levels in our club. Gordy Lane was a four-time NHL Stanley Cup champion Defenseman for the New York Islanders. In the club, they decided Gordy would visit with all the teams and help the coaches with his extensive knowledge and NHL experience. I was a little nervous when he came to my practice. In the two hours he spent with me and my team, I learned more from that guy about how defense works in hockey than in five years of reading and studying the game. Why is that? He was a guy who had been in the trenches. He knew it all.

Finding deep mentors like Gordy Lane is not easy. When we seek them out, we must be certain we're defending against getting advice from the wrong people. We tend to like advice from people who tell us *what we want to hear* – not *what we need to know*.

Our mentors should not necessarily be our friends or relatives. We want someone who tells us the truth, giving a clear pathway and understanding of the commitment involved, and who has a detailed background "in the trenches" of whatever their expertise is, at the highest levels.

I've had many times in my life when I did the wrong thing because when I was younger, I sought advice from people who told me what I wanted to hear. This is a natural process because it can allow you to take the easy path and validate the misconceptions you have perceived about your unique viewpoint.

There is more than one way to "skin the cat" and just because you found a way that works doesn't mean it is the best way. What works today may not work tomorrow; what works today may not be what moves you to the next level. You must constantly innovate to evolve both personally and professionally.

Seeking advice: the 10% factor

Be careful who you seek advice from, and know the source thoroughly. People who spew ideologies are no match for those who possess true knowledge.

Dr. Jordan Peterson said, "Ideologies are substitutes for true knowledge, and ideologues are always dangerous when they come to power because a simple minded I-know-it-all approach is no match for the complexity of our existence."

How do you know from whom to get advice? I've had many times in my life where I thought I was getting advice from good, quality resources, but it turned out not to be true. In fact, in one instance, it was not only terrible advice, but the "advisor" was a criminal. Oh, I thought he was the greatest guy in the world, but had I taken the time to do some research on his previous 20 years, I would have known right away that there were chinks in his armor. Those things come down to looking at someone's history. And I believe in people who have been "in the trenches."

When seeking advice, I always like to use what I call the 10% factor. In any given profession, only the top 10% are deeply experienced with an extensive in-the-trenches record. Furthermore, there are times when finding the top 10% is not good enough, and it's imperative to seek the top 1%. Sometimes, these decisions can be a matter of life and death.

My older daughter graduated from high school with honors in the spring of 2010. I'm not sure how this happened, coming from me, but she was an intellectual prodigy who thrived in academics and was awarded a full academic scholarship to the University of South Carolina. Like most other 18-year-olds, she was a bright, beautiful, optimistic, and amazing young woman, full of life, headed out to conquer the world.

Midway through her first semester, she was not feeling well. She slept 14 hours a day and could not regulate her blood sugar levels. We had her come home and immediately go to the National Institute of Health, where my former wife's family had been studied for a rare endocrine disease that could potentially cause random tumors anywhere in the body.

Eventually, in life, most of us experience this. We got "the call." My vibrant young daughter had a large, serious tumor in her pancreas. Depending on the location and type, a pancreatic tumor can be fatal. The team of doctors at NIH immediately went to work by performing tests and scans to determine what type of surgery would be attempted to save my daughter's life.

Based on the location of the tumor, they concluded that the only option was to attempt a surgery called a Whipple. This complex surgery involves removing the head of the pancreas, parts of the small intestine, the gallbladder, and the bile duct. If successful, this procedure leaves one with lifelong digestive issues and the potential for a colostomy bag. They wanted to schedule the surgery immediately.

At the surgery consult, none of us were comfortable with the conclusions. This was hardly what any of us could conceive of as an option, so our family went to work to seek out other specialists in pancreatic tumors. We sent my daughter's scans to several of the top medical facilities in the country.

We got an immediate call from a Dr. Richard Alexander from the University of Maryland Medical Center. We discovered that Dr.

Alexander was one of the foremost experts in the world for pancreatic tumors. Although it was risky, he felt he could remove my daughter's tumor based on the pinpoint location without doing the Whipple procedure, leaving enough of the pancreas to function properly.

At the consultation, Dr. Alexander said that based on my daughter's age and the full life in front of her, the Whipple procedure would leave her with a miserable existence. We were all comfortable that we had found our "in the trenches" doctor, who was clearly in an elite class. The surgery was scheduled, and he performed it to perfection. My daughter is now thriving in life with a family of her own.

When dealing with so-called experts in any challenge, always do your research on the track record. Seek out not only an expert but the best-qualified expert who has the history to prove it. The question is not just, "Who has experience?" but "Who is the best?" Apply this to all aspects of your life, and you will maximize your odds and percentages of success over time. Had we listened to the initial so-called experts in my daughter's case, her life would have never been the same.

Do you want to go to war with a battlefield commander who is on their fourth tour or an entry-level sergeant who just came out of boot camp? An experienced soldier can be the difference between life and death on the battlefield, and the same rule applies to the rest of life. Although not much compares to a battle situation where your life is on the line, depending on the leadership and the guy next to you, it is imperative that you take this mentality and apply it to all challenges in life. Who we seek advice from, who we choose to guide us and assist us, are life-changing decisions.

Someone who has been "in the trenches" means someone with a deep level of experience. However, it does not mean they have never failed. Actually, I prefer getting advice from someone who has seen the bad side of their expertise and had a chance to work through it.

Watch out for the Snake! Intentions

There is a significant difference between unintended consequences and bad intentions. If you ever see a situation where someone has ill-will or bad intentions directed towards other people, run the other way. These people are called Snakes and unfortunately in today's world they are everywhere.

However, do not confuse a Snake with an individual that unknowingly caused an unintended consequence. This happens all of the time in the business world and has happened to me on several occasions. Someone who caused an unintended consequence is not a Snake. The way to tell is to see how they managed their unintended situation. What did they do to resolve it? How did they handle those individuals affected? Did they learn from it? Did it lead to a lesson that made them better for it moving forward?

The challenge of trust

We all find ourselves in situations where we need guidance and support. Whether it's making an important life decision or seeking advice on a specific problem, asking for advice can be helpful. However, not all advice is created equal, and knowing who to trust when seeking guidance is crucial.

We seek advice from close friends and family members because we already trust them. We know they care about us. The problem is they may know little or nothing about what we're asking. The first person I asked about owning real estate as an investment was my father, because he was an intelligent, trustworthy, experienced business person. He told me to avoid real estate, warning me of all the headaches and hassles.

I took his advice to heart – for a while – until one day a light went off in my head. As great as my father is, he had almost no real estate experience whatsoever. Why did I think he could guide me in this?

This doesn't mean I ignored what my father told me, but that I looked at it within its context. His was advice from someone who wanted to spare me from troubles. The people who love you the most will always try to protect you. In their mind they are doing the right thing. Instead, I needed advice from a "big fish" in real estate, someone who had experienced the procedures, benefits, downsides, and upsides of real estate investment, someone who could tell me how to get started and how to succeed.

Still, it's no secret that trusting others can be difficult. We often struggle to discern who to trust, relying on personal biases and preferences rather than objective criteria. For example, we tend to trust those we like on a personal level, even if it may not be to our advantage. We innately tend to trust people who remind us of ourselves. We admire confidence and attractiveness and associate these things with honesty. This tendency is evident in various contexts, such as seeking advice from colleagues or choosing service providers like a landscaper or contractor.

Six questions to determine trustworthiness

"You are either lifetime or you're one time."

– J.T. Foxx

When seeking advice, it's crucial to evaluate the trustworthiness of the person offering it. To do this, consider asking yourself the following six questions:

Is this a person of integrity?

Integrity is the cornerstone of trust. A person of integrity is honest, has honorable values, consistently lives by those values, and strives to do the right thing. Assessing someone's integrity may require some investigation. Seek references from past employers or colleagues, check their standing with organizations like the Better Business Bureau, and search for online reviews. Remember, the best predictor of future trustworthiness is past trustworthiness. If the answer to this question is "no," it's best to steer clear and save yourself the trouble and heartache of trusting someone who isn't worthy of your trust.

I'd like to note here that one of the measures of integrity is: "What are you doing when no one is watching?"

I would say that 90% of the effort I have put into my personal success was when I was alone behind closed doors. It was not to impress anyone else or anyone watching. Learn to impress yourself! You will find this true of all elite achievers. We'll dwell more on this in the chapter "I Stand Alone."

Does the person display competence?

Competence is another essential factor to consider when evaluating trustworthiness. It involves having the demonstrated knowledge and skills to perform a specific task. Look for individuals who have a history of success in relation to the goal or task at hand. Be aware of the difference between confidence and competence. While someone may talk a good game, their past is a better indicator of their actual abilities. Ensure the person has the skills necessary to get the job done. Remember also that a past failure is not in itself a dealbreaker when it comes to confidence. If the person learned from their failure, overcame it or pivoted their performance in a way that shows growth, this can be a sign of remarkable character.

Is the person dependable?

Dependability is crucial when considering who to trust. Evaluate whether the person consistently follows through on their commitments. While nobody is perfect, a reliable individual will meet deadlines, show up on time for appointments, and do what they say they will do. Consider their history of reliability and accountability. Even if someone passes the first two questions, if they can't be depended upon to complete tasks or follow through, it may not be wise to trust them. How you do one thing is how you do everything!

Does the person care?

Passion for the subject of advice plays a significant role in determining trustworthiness. We've already established that seeking advice from those who love us can be problematic because their desire is to protect us. So when we seek advice about improving, we often have to look for "caring" of another type. When Gordy Lane came to coach my hockey players, I didn't imagine that he "cared" for us all like family or that this was a situation of lifetime friendship, and it would have been ridiculous to do so. But what Mr. Lane did care about was the sport, the abilities of the athletes, and imparting his knowledge in a helpful way. His commitment to his purpose was obvious.

A trustworthy individual will demonstrate open communication, transparency, and authenticity in their dealings with you. And yes, in certain situations, expertise and reputation take precedence over personal connection. You may get the best advice from people you do not particularly like. Don't let your emotions override rational judgment when evaluating trustworthiness.

Is the person loyal?

When it comes to evaluating all the above character traits of trustworthiness there is an intangible factor related to loyalty. I have learned that the greatest relationships come with an impeccable level of loyalty. Observe how long they maintain their relationships. Who did they work with from 10, 20, or 30 years ago? Did they stick with colleagues and allies during difficult tough times?

Is the person healthy and fit?

Show me a fit man or woman and I'll show you someone who is on the success track. Why would you take advice or invest with someone who does not have the ability to take care of their most precious asset, themselves?

There are no guarantees!
"Mistakes don't define you—they refine you."
--Dave Ramsey

With everything said in this chapter, there is no way in life to ensure anything will turn out as it appears. You will make mistakes and misjudgments. The greatest scam artists like Bernie Madoff and Sam Friedman and, on a personal level, the guy who scammed me for a million, were all flamboyant personalities whose skill sets reeled in even the greatest of due diligence investors. Most of the investors who get caught up in these types of scams are brought into the scam by another trustworthy investor whom they know. "If it's good enough for them, I'm sure it's a great thing."

The fallacy is that you assume that since others invested millions that it's secure and someone else has done the detailed due diligence. My greatest lesson is to not only trust your own due diligence but be willing to ask tough questions and walk away upon red flag answers. This is tough to do when everyone else is jumping in. This is not limited to investing as you can be scammed out of just about anything by a sophisticated Snake operator. Many times, this could be someone you know very well.

The conclusion is that it is imperative to look past the emotion of a relationship and get down to the facts and track record. We are all guilty of being drawn to people for the wrong reasons. The emotional component of that is often enough to reel you in just because you feel good about the personality you are dealing with. Keep in mind that this tactic is how all the greatest con artists in history built their Snake pits.

As careful as you may be, occasionally you will be duped, and people will wrong you no matter how perfectly you vet someone or something. This is simply part of the growing process in life, and my favorite line of when a deal or relationship goes bad is, "...*NEXT!*" Put it behind you and be better for it.

Vindictiveness will rob you of your future.
Success is the greatest revenge.

CHAPTER SIX

SUCCESS DEFINED

"Success is not owned, it's rented – and that rent is due every day."
--Rory Vaden

Success can be defined in a thousand different ways. Your personal definition of success is directly correlated to your core beliefs and internal knowledge of your history and experiences in life. Even the greatest philosophers, teachers, and self-help gurus could not agree on a single definition because success will never mean exactly the same thing to everyone. Therefore, we cannot put a specific meaning on success and expect it to work for everyone. Rather, we should talk about the general facets of success and see how each facet can be shaped, like the facets of a gem, to create exactly the right cut of success for each individual.

From my viewpoint after studying successful people for more than 40 years along with my own experiences, this is what I believe success to mean:

Spending your life on a series of worthy causes and achievements aligned with ethical and moral practices that build your inner core to yield confidence, self-esteem, contentment, peace of mind, and serenity.

You do not need to necessarily feel good about who you are today… you should focus on the evolution of who you can become tomorrow. It's never too late. Your life should be like a hurricane eyewall. It keeps reinventing itself.

Success can also be described as putting your head on your pillow each night knowing you're a person of high integrity and intent. You sleep very well! You also wake up excited to face each day, with no dread for what the day holds for you. Everyone has problems and challenges to deal with. The trick is to create "good" problems caused by your success and opportunities in life. Success is as challenging as failure, but it is a challenge that we are glad to face. The beautiful thing is you get to choose which challenges you prefer in life.

You may have noticed that "money" was not included in my definition of success. So, let's clear this up right now. Money is a *result* of success and a subset of the concept. Chase success, and money will chase you. Chase money, and you will be running your whole life. Money equals freedom; this is why we want it. Money is a trailing indicator. It's the residue of your success. Food for thought: money fixes every problem except the one inside you.

> *"Money isn't everything but it's reasonably close*
> *to oxygen on the gotta-have-it scale."*
> --Zig Ziglar

Success derives from a series of wins and losses. Nobody wins all the time. All you must do is engage in daily actions that produce more wins than losses. As you learn more about the ladder in later chapters, you will see that you can climb your daily ladder by taking inventory at the end of each day.

Did my actions today take me up a rung towards the path of my dreams, or did my actions take me down a rung on the path to regret?

Every time I get a win, I think of it as going in my pocket, and there it stays forever. However, so do losses…so the trick is to fill your pockets with wins.

Many losses are simply setbacks – it's all about what you do with your losses that matter. Everyone is going to have losses. Do you become a victim to them, or do you reengage, take a lesson, and keep on going? I'm in a high-net-worth investor group full of super-wealthy people – with the recent rise in interest rates, a lot of these people are real estate people, and the interest rates are kicking their asses. They were extremely successful people, but they were sure singing the blues yesterday! Everybody will endure losses. Everybody has problems. It is critical, however, to categorize a loss for what it actually is. Our successes can put us in a position to endure losses. So, do not lose your perspective of the opportunity you created to produce a loss.

If losses accumulate, they are more difficult to get out of your pocket, and you carry them around with you for a lifetime. I can't emphasize enough the power of accumulating wins daily to launch you up the ladder.

These are simple things in life like going to the gym, eating healthily, making someone else feel great, working on or completing that project, and so on. The more wins you accumulate, the more your subconscious mind becomes receptive to success and the more likely you are to repeat these positive behaviors. In fact, over time, they will become automatic.

Mark Manson has a book titled, *The Subtle Art of Not Giving a F*ck*. In that book, he talks about negative feedback loops where you're constantly beating yourself up because you're not doing the things you should be doing. When you do that, you're going down your ladder. You're making yourself feel bad because you're not executing, and you are continually reinforcing that behavior. However, the more you engage in this process of accumulating wins, the more likely you are to produce a positive feedback loop and propel up your ladder. The wins give you a push up the ladder, and the losses will shove you down. Which is the harder path with the most resistance? A push up or a shove down? Prepare for battle – or you will be doomed to the path of least resistance!

Daily wins eventually translate to weekly wins, then monthly wins and yearly wins. In order to climb the Ladder of the Cheetah, you must get yearly wins, which emanate from the percentage of the 365 days of the year that you execute your daily wins. We will talk more later about this concept.

At the end of the day all that really matters to create true success in life is how you feel about yourself! Therefore, you should spend the majority of your time on yourself and becoming the you that you always dreamed of! In order to achieve this, you must accept that all of your excuses are lies.

"You can fool all the people some of the time and some of the people all the time, but you cannot fool all the people all the time."
--Abraham Lincoln

Look at characteristics instead of laws

As you move into your lifelong journey of continued learning, you will discover that many of the authors of books, speakers at events, masterminds, or reels on social media bombard you with rules and laws. They tell us, "Follow these 12 rules of success; focus on these five habits; or master these ten laws!" Although, in many cases, the content contained in these rules and laws may be valuable and necessary for your learning process, they don't actually get you to move in the right direction and, in many cases, can set you back on your climb to the top. I am not a fan of rules and laws about "what we must do."

Often, successful people like to tell us about rules and laws they believe one must follow in order to experience similar success.

Brian Tracy wrote a series called *The Universal Laws of Success and Achievement.*

The founder of GoDaddy, Bob Parsons, also has a remarkable success story. His company was going under, and he put every last penny he had into one Super Bowl commercial and just completely turned it around. He, too, has sixteen rules for success.

Stephen Covey has *The 7 Habits of Highly Effective People*.

These rules and laws are all relevant content, but here's what I find wrong about these sorts of lists. People listen to all these advice podcasts or attend these seminars where they hear all these rules. "You gotta follow these ten rules if you want to be successful!"

What happens is that while you're sitting there, your emotions get involved. You're thinking, "Oh this is great! I've got to do these things!" What happens, and I would say this happens a hundred percent of the time, is that you come away from these lessons for a few days with these thoughts in mind of what you must do. But you soon realize that you're not really following those laws. Nobody does immediately.

When that happens, it creates a perceived failure that turns into a negative feedback loop. After you see these rules and laws, you actually start to feel worse about yourself because you found out about all the things you haven't been doing and won't be doing, among other things that you couldn't figure out how to do.

No one can follow the monumental task of aligning a new life of rules and laws in an instant. You're only going to make yourself feel worse. Let's dig a little deeper as to why rules and laws can actually *set you back* on your climb up the ladder if you do not have a plan for following through in a way that reflects your unique needs. Again, I'm not against the content of these rules and laws; it's extremely valuable information. I want you to use the content you learn in these rules and laws, knowing that it will take a lengthy time to initialize and integrate it through studying how successful people have done so.

There are no shortcuts up the ladder. We go rung by rung with periodic steps backward, and sometimes, it takes years to reach a new height on the ladder.

When you are bombarded with following these rules or implementing these laws, we initially think that this is easy. "I'll just do those things, and life will be wonderful!" Unfortunately, it does not work that way.

Even though we have a breakthrough in our learning, the result is failure in the execution. Therefore, we regress back to where we were. We may even quit pursuing the rules and laws because our ingrained habits that don't conform to those rules and laws are impossible to change or conquer without a persistent, long-term, dedicated effort.

The emotion of the moment will not overcome the logic of the future. You'll find it exceedingly difficult to change any of your ingrained habits of who you are, what you are, what you think, or your subconscious mind just by attending a seminar or even reading a book. None of it is going to change in a week or two. It's just like a New Year's resolution, and why most people give up on their New Year's resolution by January 2nd!

To move forward with making significant changes in your life, you must first understand that such change can take years. The only way to approach your long-term growth potential is with a resilient mindset that is prepared for battle daily.

Instead of focusing on the rules and laws of highly successful people you need to focus on the characteristics of highly successful people and slowly tend toward them, until you make them your characteristics as well.

How do you do this? Employ your Great Observer! You must emulate the actions and activities of those you want to be like. Hang out with them, learn from them, read about them, ask frequent questions. Observe their characteristics and slowly over time engage in the same thinking and activities that they do.

Through this process, you will not "find" yourself, but rather, you will "create" yourself. Virtually everything that has led me up my ladder came from observing and learning from mentors and allies. This requires me to question everything and be open-minded. What I *think* I know may not be what I *need* to know. And it's not just leadership and success you learn from, either. It's also the failures and recovery of the ones you wish to emulate that will teach you.

The characteristics of success

Only after years of learning will you tend in the direction of highly successful people. The best you can hope for is to tend in a better direction of how you think and what you do.

Let's have a look at what those characteristics are. As we move onto the characteristics of highly successful people, I'd like you to do a personal inventory of how you would rate yourself in each of these areas. You may feel that you are already engaged in some and feel that some areas need an initial starting point. Remember your goal is to tend in the direction of each of these characteristics over a lengthy period.

As I said, there are no hard rules or laws that will magically make this happen for you. It's a slow climb, step by step, that eventually allows you to look back at your former self and clearly recognize the progress you have made climbing your ladder. This is a process that requires a specific duration of time; in most cases, we are talking years. If you recognize this, you can avoid falling into the negative feedback loop. When you have a setback in any of these areas, just view it as a reset and opportunity to get it right moving forward. As the successes build over time, you will then understand how the process works, and the positive outcomes will accelerate.

These characteristics are the ones that I have personally observed and/or experienced over the past 40 years. The one thing I would like to share is that this list has never changed because the same things that made a human a successful human being on this planet a thousand years ago are the same things that will make a human being successful a thousand years from now. Why? Because as described earlier, we are biological beings that have an embedded DNA system that dictates through our emotional brains for this to be true. You cannot and will not change human nature.

I learned a little tidbit from Tim Grover many years ago. I was at one of his speaking engagements and put a list on the screen. The list had no numbers on it. It was just ten topics, listed in no particular order. He then explained that as soon as you put a numeric application to the list the list then is perceived in importance by the order that they are listed. Since all ten of his topics to discuss had equal importance and also the fact that different topics may have been more important to certain people vs. others, I learned that day to accept content in the order of the value to me. You should do the same.

As I move through the list of the 18 characteristics of highly successful people, I want you to do your own evaluation of the order of importance. However, I must violate my mentor Tim Grover's concept on this list as in this case there is one characteristic that is the most important to any and all types of success. The rest of the list's interpretation related to the order of importance is up to you.

Here are the characteristics of successful people.

#1 - **Health and wellness**. Health is wealth! One hour of workouts to feel good for the next 23 hours? Sounds like a good deal to me. To maintain a consistent upward climb, maintaining a vigorous health and wellness routine is non-negotiable. This is a lifestyle that will span your lifetime, not a some-of-the-time thing. Your body must function like a well-oiled machine so that it can be in perfect alignment with your mind. A mind cannot function in turbo mode without a partnership with its body. A Ferrari won't run on 87 octane fuel! Without an elite level of health and wellness, what good are all of the other characteristics on this list going to do for you? Not much, when you're sick, tired, lazy, less productive, disinterested, and deteriorating daily. Your diet is not only what you eat. It's what you watch, listen to, read, and also the people you associate with. Your mental diet is just as critical as your physical diet. They must be in committed collaboration with each other. Do not limit the potential of what you were put on this earth to achieve.

Faith. The core belief, "If I do enough of the right things, enough of the time, over a long period of time, good outcomes are coming my way." What you perceive is what you believe.

Resilience and Discipline: The ability to adjust, pivot, realign, and restart, even in the most adverse situations. Changing directions is not quitting. Optimize speed by being resourceful. This is the number one common characteristic of all Cheetahs, Falcons and Alpha Lions.

Ethics/Morals: The foundation of your inner moral core will be built and developed on the initial stages of your climb. I will present more on this topic in a later chapter.

Relationships/Loyalty: Associate with only allies who are willing to go to war with you, and you to war with them. Deep-seated trust in the ethics and goodness of another individual and your ability to deliver the same will serve you well over decades of time. Provide value first! Those who do not fit the mold must be eliminated. Look at yourself like a brand. The number one thing a brand needs to be successful is trust.

Sales/Negotiation: Basic knowledge of sales and negotiation is required for high level success, but it is just as important for defense. You must have the ability to sniff out a Snake and not be manipulated or scammed. The Snakes' world is expanding!

Finance/Investing: Finance is not just about making money, it's about keeping and growing your money. I'm amazed at how many income earners spend no time educating themselves on financial management. Here's a clue: The money you make is not your money...the money *your money makes* is your money.

Self-Development: Nothing of lasting value will emerge without spending time on self-learning. The average CEO of an S&P 500 company reads up to 60 books a year! With the availability of Audible and book summaries, you have no excuse not to grow your knowledge daily. If this is new for you, commit to just 15 minutes daily, and you will be amazed at the new you that evolves.

Selfishness: Taking care of yourself is the greatest gift you can give to anyone else. When you are better, they are better for it! Write a contract with yourself, and don't negotiate it.

Showing up: Every time you show up for anything, you are potentially one relationship away from changing your life forever. I have never shown up for anything that did not provide some form of lesson, growth, and/or opportunity. Sometimes, showing up teaches us where not to be!

Failure is an opportunity: How many times have you heard "failure is not an option?" In truth, failure is a valuable option. Failure is simply the opportunity to learn how to grow and improve. Fail often when young, and be wise and knowledgeable when old.

Accountability/Responsibility: Be the "go to" person in your world. Take accountability and responsibility for everything both in and out of your control.

Risk: The foundation of a growth mindset. We'll discuss this further in later chapters

Respect/Kindness/Gratitude: Not all high achievers are what I would call nice people, but they are kind people who keep their perspective. How many people in this world would change places with you right now?

Time: This is your most precious commodity that must not be squandered. We will cover this in depth.

Logic: All high achievers have the ability to apply logic over emotion. When it logically doesn't fit or make sense, learn to say "no" often. Develop uncommon common sense!

Massive action. All elite performers apply the WINN principle: When If Not Now? They consistently go all-in. Procrastination, hesitation, and laziness are Sheep characteristics.

Knowledge of history: Knowledge of the past predicts the future. This tool is used to avoid repeating mistakes of the past and thrive on historical victories of earlier times. Your knowledge of history will have broad implications over your lifetime.

As you move along in life you will learn that things are never as good as they appear, and things are never as bad as they appear. For every great moment of euphoria, there will be a moment of crisis. There's nobody that lives a life of daily euphoria. Only children believe that someday, every day will be one of euphoria.

To me, a state of euphoria is having inner peace, contentment, and confidence. That's what euphoria means to me now. Whereas twenty years ago, getting a Ferrari was euphoria. There's no amount of contentment or inner peace that you can buy. It's never about material things. All the greater things in life cannot be bought, and those are the things that matter the most. Your relationships. Your quality of being a parent. Your ethics and morals. What you're doing for other people. How other people in your allies group perceive you. How you fit into society and what benefits you can provide to the betterment of community.

What we want is serenity. We want to have a joyful presence of our inner self and our surroundings. We want to wake up in the morning motivated, driven, and ready to go because you are a joyful person. If you have serenity in your life, it's hard to describe what it means, but if you have created every aspect of your life within your control to be flowers and roses, you're going to be pretty content. But you must create all that. Nobody can do that for you. It's all up to you to create that, and it takes a lifetime.

I don't think anybody in their twenties, thirties, or forties could grasp what end-of-life serenity means or looks like because they are in the middle of their learning process. This is perfectly normal and brings in the faith quality of successful people. They're back and forth on failures and achievements. When people age, the things that used to bring us down slowly start to disappear if you do all the right actions to climb your ladder.

When I talk to younger people, I want to convey that my plan is a 50-year plan; you're going to find your greatest moments of euphoria way after you thought you would. You can't change who you are in two weeks or even two months. You need years of slowly getting better in these categories. You need to have a general understanding of how successful people became successful.

I will share with you the *habits* in which successful people engage; learn to implement these in your daily life, and you'll find yourself living those "laws" and "rules" that everyone talks about naturally and effortlessly.

But first, let's clarify something. There is an exception for one type of laws and one set of rules that *do* always apply, and rightfully so. They are the Laws of Human Nature and the Unwritten Rules.

Building a successful life is not about reinventing the wheel; it's about finding a wheel you can roll with.

CHAPTER SEVEN

HUMAN NATURE

What lies behind us and what lies before us
is nothing compared to what lies within us.
-- Ralph Waldo Emerson

If you think you can change the Laws of Human Nature, you will learn in short order that you are playing a losing game. In fact, when you violate the Laws of Human Nature, you are guaranteeing a bad outcome eventually. Throughout history, human societies have grappled with complex questions about human behavior, ethics, and the nature of our species. In this chapter, we will explore how the Laws of Human Nature have shaped the course of history, from the ancient civilizations of Mesopotamia to the modern world. By delving into these historical narratives, we can gain valuable insights into the timeless principles that govern human behavior.

One of the fundamental principles of ancient humans was the concept of reciprocity—an eye for an eye, a tooth for a tooth. This principle recognized that human beings are inherently driven by a sense of fairness and the desire for retribution when wronged. Then came the Golden Rule, which speaks to a fundamental aspect of human nature: empathy. It acknowledges that we are social beings who are capable of understanding and sharing the feelings of others. Throughout history, societies that embraced this principle tended to be more harmonious and cooperative, as individuals recognized the interconnectedness of their fates.

Tribal Law

Throughout history, the Laws of Human Nature have been a driving force behind the evolution of societies, the development of ethics, and the creation of legal systems. As we navigate the complexities of the modern world, it is essential to continue exploring and appreciating the Laws of Human Nature that have shaped our past. By doing so, we can make more informed decisions about our future and strive to create a society that aligns with the timeless principles inherent in our nature as human beings.

Long before there were police departments or security systems, human beings understood how to keep each other in line. Tribes, clans, small villages – all of these places needed people to conform to behavior that was best for the group. Doing what was best for the group resulted in enjoying the benefits of the group – companionship, safety, and assistance. And if a member was not willing to contribute their fair share, they were corrected somehow by the group. The corrections could have been as simple as, "If you don't till the fields with us, you don't get your share of the grain," or as brutal as, "If you don't till the fields with us, you can spend your winters in the forest with the hungry wolves."

This is called "tribal law" and it exists even today, in groups of friends or corporate cultures or anywhere in the world where a group comes together for an agreed purpose. Tribal law happens organically because we are social animals. Tribal law is the most basic form of human nature: *If you don't contribute to the group's goals, you don't get to enjoy the group's benefits.*

Humans have been around for at least five million years. In that time, yes, we evolved both physically and mentally. We now possess a higher brain that has evolved over millions of years. Through education and better nutrition, we have developed the capacity to have a superior body compared to our ancient ancestors. Both of those are assets that we, as modern-day humans, can use to our advantage.

However, what I want you to clearly understand is what has not changed. The same things that made a human develop success, contentment, confidence, and inner peace a million years ago are the same things that make us that way today. This is because of our biological makeup. We are a species of logic and emotion, and the same process of using our brains to execute our thinking to perform daily functions and activities has not changed.

We are animals that carry with us six basic human emotions: happiness, sadness, anger, surprise, fear, and disgust, and then within these emotions are 27 other subset emotions. When it comes to the Laws of Human Nature, you must accept that these emotions are built into who you are, and any outward expression of any one of these emotions is perfectly normal and to be expected. Society today tries to dictate that acting on certain emotions is unacceptable.

I have never met anyone who, from time to time, does not display these six basic emotions – and on a regular basis. Do not let society dictate to you that you are not a normal human being! A little side note here: Do you know what human sub-emotion elicits the largest dopamine response? According to Human Biologist Gary Brecka, it's authenticity. What does that tell you about the importance of ethics and morals to your overall well-being?

Your acceptance of the Laws of Human Nature will allow you to be content with yourself and not beat yourself up when you express normal behavioral reactions. Yes, we can learn from how we act and learn to control our emotions to the best of our abilities, but each one of us is unique in how our emotional brains work.

For example, I have had attention issues my whole life that caused me serious problems as a child. One of the characteristics of ADD is to have a reactionary personality. Folks like me want things resolved and resolved *now*. This characteristic was detrimental to me in relationships and also caused short-term bad decision-making. So, knowing that about myself, I learned to consciously be aware of when I am about to react too quickly and put a pause on that reaction the best I can.

We all have our little glitches in our personalities that can affect us both positively and negatively. My advice is to learn who you are, understand yourself, and improve the things that you want to control. What I do not want you to do is beat yourself on the top of the head every time you display an emotion that you wish you hadn't. Learn about yourself and train your mind to be in control of your emotions in the manner that you prefer.

When you engage in an emotion that may be to someone else's detriment, recognize it, be accountable, and get it right the next time. It's okay to explain yourself in an apologetic manner. This is required with unintended projected emotions. "I'm sorry" can mean a lot, as opposed to sitting on your pride when you recognize that your intent was misguided.

Unwritten Rules

The best way to describe the unwritten rules is this: eventually, no one gets away with anything related to human nature, and specifically when addressing morals and ethics. Life has a way of evening out both the good and the bad as well as the euphoric and tragic. The unwritten rules are rules enforced by our natural human behaviors based on what's acceptable and what's not.

One of my favorite examples of unwritten rules is the ability to fight in the game of hockey. Fights in hockey generally occur because of the unwritten rules.

Of course, you have the rules of the game, with two linesmen and two referees to enforce those rules. However, when a call is missed, a bad call is made, or a player takes a cheap dirty shot at an opposing player or goalie, this is where the enforcers come into the game. It is an unwritten rule that you do not go after goalies or star players with head checks, open ice hits, or any type of intent to injure activity. If you do, you can be assured that at some time during the game, the enforcers are coming after you. Every team in the NHL has at least one enforcer (fighter) on the roster.

A lot of people ask why fighting is allowed in hockey, and the answer is that the ability to have the unwritten rules enforced by the players makes the players more accountable for their actions, and it is overall better for the game.

This same concept applies to all areas of life. Unwritten rules are everywhere in life and can lift you to new heights when followed and be detrimental when not. If you do something irresponsible, eventually, that irresponsibility will come at you with a negative impact.

If you are behaving badly in any capacity, the Laws of Human Nature enforcers are eventually going to catch up with you and deal with you accordingly. Dr Jordan Peterson said that in his 30 years of therapy sessions, he never once met anyone who got away with anything, *eventually*.

It's the karma of the universe. If you do things you shouldn't be doing, if you're behaving in ways you shouldn't behave, there are consequences for everything eventually.

This is why I urge you, in spite of daily temptation, to learn to discipline yourself to behave in a morally ethical manner to the best of your ability. For the times when you don't (and it happens to all of us), I advise you to learn from the unwritten rule that is eventually going to correct you. By recognizing this process, you can again begin to build that positive feedback loop to your mind that will slowly elevate you up your ladder.

Time is your friend

You'll find it difficult to change any of your ingrained habits of who you are, what you are, what you think, or your subconscious mind just by attending a seminar or even reading a book. None of it is going to change in a week or two. Change is a trending process, a long-term process of repetitive behaviors. It involves ingraining new muscle and mind memories. Understanding a new side of the game. Practice, rehearse, repeat. It takes months and years, not days.

After my freshman year at Maryland, I was in the bottom six players on the golf team. I knew I had to do something to get my average score down about one shot to get onto the starting travel team. So, I went on a mission to do that. But that mission involved intense practice, more rounds played and less party time to up my game. I spent more time in these aggressive actions for an entire year.

Note that part of my process was cutting back on the bad habit of drinking and partying; remember, it's not only what you do but also what you *don't* do that elevates you to success. Two months in, or three months in, no matter how hard I practiced, I wasn't going to go out and have that average score. But over that year, I was able to do that and went on to make the starting team.

Where were you two years ago? Where were you five years ago? I don't care about a month ago, and you shouldn't either because you won't make significant changes in a month. It takes years to do this stuff.

I'd like this to be taught as a person's evolution - to slowly become more like the people who have those characteristics that you want to have. The people who you consider highly successful didn't just read books on how to become successful and do it in a week. It would take that successful person ten years of blood, sweat, and tears to become the person you admire today. They have been in the trenches and have become deeply experienced. You will need to do the same. Furthermore, you rarely see the effort as the effort is mostly internal and behind closed doors.

Change your nature: 11 life-altering habits

Now that you know the long-term growth principles of highly successful people, as promised, I will share with you the path to the results. This will be the easiest avenue to emulate these people with your daily actions. Bestselling author and clinical psychologist Adam Grant did a long-term study of successful people and concluded that you do not have to have special talents or be a wunderkind to achieve success.

It's all about consistently applying your knowledge and implementing the 11 life altering habits listed below on a daily basis. Learn these and again be aware of your tendencies to improve these thoughts and actions over time. Remember, your aim is not about complying with laws or rules in a day and becoming a brand-new person (that's not possible); rather your aim is to internalize these and make progress on each of them for years to come.

Seek Discomfort. Pursuing discomfort sets you on a faster path to growth. If you want to get it right, it has to feel wrong first.

Set a mistake budget. To encourage trial and error, set a goal for the minimum number of mistakes you make daily or weekly. When you expect to stumble, you ruminate about it less and improve more.

Seek advice, not feedback. As we discussed in the chapter "In the Trenches," seeking advice is imperative to success. Feedback is backward-looking. It leads people to criticize you or cheer for you. Advice is forward-looking. It leads people to coach you. Always ask, "What's the one thing I could do better next time?"

Figure out who to trust. We already know you must avoid the Snakes. Trust your intuition and decide what information to absorb and what to let go. Make sure your coaches have relevant expertise and know you well. Make sure they have your best interest in mind and soul. Great coaches can be expensive…PAY IT! They are worth the money!

Strive for excellence, not perfection. We already addressed that perfection is a losing game. Progress comes from maintaining high standards, but always be aware that we all have shortcomings that we must accept. Identify where you truly need the best and where you can settle for good enough.

You are your own last judge. It's better to disappoint others than to disappoint yourself. Remember, you are always the #1 project. Before you release something into the world, make sure it represents the best of you. Are you proud of it? If not, it's not ready!

Turn the daily grind into a daily source of joy. We call this learning to love the battle because you will learn to love the results. To maintain your passion, set up fun skill-building challenges. Make everything a game. Eventually what was hard becomes routine.

When stuck, back up to move forward. Resilience requires adaptation, adjustments, and the ability to change paths when you get stuck vs. quitting. This can feel like a setback, but it's the launching pad for a new direction.

Teach what you learn. I call this sharing the wealth. The best way to master what you learn is to teach it to others. This reinforces your knowledge to a higher level.

Open doors for underrated or overlooked people. Create systems that create opportunities for everyone, not just the gifted or talented. The more people you take with you on your journey, the more successful you will be.

Engage in mental time travel. When you struggle to appreciate your progress, look back at yourself from several years ago. It's difficult to see short-term progress, but with an evaluation of years, it's easy to see how far you have come.

Bad habits are easy to develop and hard to live with…
good habits are hard to develop and easy to live with.
--Orrin Woodward

CHAPTER EIGHT

LEARNING BEGINS WHEN EDUCATION ENDS

"If the path to billions were in books,
every librarian would be a billionaire."
--Warren Buffet

WINN: When, If Not Now?

Lifelong continued learning is one of the pillars of your ladder's foundation. Let's get one thing perfectly clear: learning does not mean sitting in a classroom. Consider your formal schooling "education" and everything else as "learning" because the type of learning I am talking about is the lessons life will teach you and the associated preparedness you have to face up to those challenges. Very few of the skills required for real-world success are ever taught in school. In the Introduction, I mentioned the old saying: The "A" students end up working for the "C" students!

Uncreative thinking and behavior are taught in our modern education system, which wants only to create more Sheep. If you look at Falcons, Cheetahs, and Alpha Lions in the real world, you'll find that many of them were bad students and had significant troubles in school, lacked confidence, and even had undiagnosed and untreated learning disabilities. Yet look where they are now.

How often does our education system teach students about the basics of finance and investing? When was the last time you had a class on developing great relationships and loyalty? I've never seen a curriculum that teaches responsibility, work ethic, or entrepreneurship. What about marriage and parenting? How about the 50-year plan that covers the several phases of your life? All the above will require us to keep learning and growing for our entire lives. I like to call it "learning while you are earning!"

Too many people finish school and consider the learning phase of their lives complete when, in reality it's just the beginning. More than 80% of high school graduates will never read a self-education or self-help book after receiving their diploma. This is simply astounding when it is one of the pillars of all 1% Achievers. In fact, the 1% Achievers read or listen to dozens of books annually.

Just like all other phases of success, continued learning requires structure, regiment, and discipline. Self-esteem arises from the accumulation of consistent small positive behaviors. As Zig Ziglar says, this can take you from a wandering generality to a meaningful specific.

When people begin self-learning, the first thing that happens is those certain ideas "hit home." *Oh no, I don't do that. Oh, I should be doing that*! For a while, we may actually feel worse about ourselves. The more we learn, the more we realize that we're not like that successful person with their successful philosophy for achievement. Shit, I just pissed away ten years! The older you are, the more likely you are to be overwhelmed by wasted years, and then the less likely you are to follow through if you take the wrong attitude. But it's never too late! I've had to learn many lessons over the decades of my life, and I'm grateful for all of them. They got me where I am today and where I will be tomorrow. Some of my greatest learning came post-50 years old!

This is why I remember WINN: When If Not Now?

If you procrastinate, postpone, or delay anything you know you should be doing, you create a loss versus a win. This means everything large and small – if you're not finishing anything in time for deadlines, obviously that's a big problem. This includes self-imposed deadlines. If I have a fantastic idea, and know I should write it down so I don't forget it – and then I *don't* write it down and I *do* forget it – that a loss for me.

Stop all this thinking of "one day" doing this or that. None of us know how long we have or what the future will bring. We must continuously execute. Successful people do this every day. Develop systems that work for you.

The problem with motivation

Knowledge without action is only potential…untapped potential is the ultimate waste of a life.

Motivation is a short-term emotional response to an outside stimulus that may have positive short-term benefits.

Of course, the simple example is a great pregame speech by a coach before an athletic event. It can create camaraderie and excitement, but eventually, when reality sets in, it does little to change longer-term outcomes.

> *"Everyone has a plan until they get punched in the mouth."*
> --Mike Tyson

When I was 26 years old, I was invited to see a motivational speaker. I initially laughed at the thought of going to something like that, figuring it must be like a cult, a room full of brainwashed zombies – or at least just a rip-off. I completely discounted the concept because I knew no one who had ever done something like that. The people I associated with at that time would consider me crazy for going to a circus like that. However, because I was invited by someone whom I highly admired, I reluctantly said yes.

I had never heard of the speaker, but he had a cool name...Zig Ziglar. For those of you who may not know who this gentleman was, let me just say this. He was one of the greatest pioneers of motivational speaking and considered a legendary storyteller. His materials and content remain mainstream and relevant today.

Little did I know that my decision to **show up** would be a life-changing event for me. We'll talk more later about the importance of **showing up.**

The setting was a small church with about one hundred people in attendance. The next two hours were the most amazing, all-encompassing presentation about life and success that anyone could ever imagine. In short, he was incredible. I walked out of the seminar walking on water and a changed man, or so I thought. Mr. Ziglar had opened my mind to another world that moved beyond the patterns of my current life.

In fact, motivation does not precede success, but *success drives motivation.* So when I left the seminar ready to set the world on fire in all aspects of my life in business, it's no surprise that just two weeks later, I was right back to my old thoughts, processes, and emotions as if I never even attended the event. What occurred a few weeks later was a big letdown. I thought I'd found the secret for a new life – but I was failing once more and beating myself up for it. This negative feedback made me feel worse about myself.

What was actually going on, though? I had learned what I was supposed to be doing to improve my outcomes in life...but I'd taken no actions to create any results.

It was at this time that I realized just how hard making changes would be, and it felt like an insurmountable task to execute. This is going to happen to you and may happen because you are reading this book. It's perfectly normal to take a step backward in the perspective of who you are when you first start the continuing learning process. You did not get to be the way you are in just a couple of weeks; it took a lifetime of misinformation and outright false beliefs. Your self-concept developed over a lifetime; therefore, the process of changing your thinking, visions, and perspectives takes years. It does not happen from attending a motivational seminar.

However, it's a start! Learning positive thinking and behaviors is a continuous process of planting the seeds of success into your subconscious mind on a consistent basis. As is with all success, this is a long, drawn-out process that will take several years to translate into changing the person who you want to be. It is absolutely critical that you clearly understand this concept or you will quit with every little setback or failure. This is why resilience is a common characteristic of all elite achievers.

10,000 hours

"Constantly improve your skills. Yesterday's world records are today's entry-level requirements."
--Billy Cox

It is a widely accepted concept that in order to become an elite expert in one profession, talent, or skill, it takes about 10,000 hours of learning, effort, and execution. That number breaks down to about 20 hours a week for 10 years. Of course, given this time allocation, this directly correlates to one's choice of any given endeavor or career, as this commitment is all-encompassing of one's time and concentrated effort into one particular specialty that we choose to pursue.

For most of us, this is correlated to our life's chosen career, business, or job. If you graduate from law school, you are certainly not an experienced attorney the day you start at your first law firm. If you choose to be an auto-mechanic, it will take you thousands of car repairs before you would be considered an expert mechanic. For most of us, this process happens as a natural evolution of ourselves as we grow and pursue our profession. Very few of us ever think of this as a 10,000-hour project, but that is exactly what it is. Because we all conform to this type of development in our lives, it's simply a natural path concentrated in only one area of expertise.

Most of us think that once we achieve expert status in one area of our lives that we have done all the work and now we're all set to conquer the world. The problem with this thinking is that our lives involve several critical other areas that also need a channeled focus.

Those areas fall into categories. They are my Fantastic Four:
- Health and Wellness
- Relationships
- Financial and Investing Literacy
- Sales and Negotiation.

What good does it do if you to make $200,000 a year and have no idea what to do with it? You can be the greatest surgeon in the country, but if you can't relate with other people, what kind of life would that be? Many of us are taken advantage of on a consistent basis because Snakes and scammers manipulate us. Getting educated in sales and negotiation allows you to recognize this immediately before the damage is done. And lastly, if you do not have your health and wellness in check, I can assure you that you are headed for a miserable existence on this planet.

What does all this mean? It's not just the 10,000 hours in your area of expertise that is required to climb the ladder to an extraordinary life. It goes beyond that, where some weekly hours must be contributed to the four other areas of learning. These areas do not require a level of expertise like your 10,000-hour profession but they do need some attention and a level of understanding so you can maximize your potential to create the best outcomes possible in your life.

The formula I like to use is to add 1,000 hours of continued learning in all four areas. 1,000 hours over 20 years means you will invest about an hour into each of these weekly, a total of 4 hours or, simply put, 30-45 minutes daily. To reach the highest levels of success and join the 1%, it is imperative that you embrace this daily habit and make it a ritual! You need not do all of these concurrently. It's perfectly okay to work on one or two of these at a time and rotate the process as you go to the other areas. Just make sure it's an ongoing process.

Do it like you love it

> *"Discipline is doing what you hate to do, but do it like you love it."*
> --Mike Tyson

Mike Tyson's quote goes way beyond the surface meaning. When you have the discipline and resilience to battle through any challenge, you not only build your inner core of self-esteem and confidence but you will also find over time what you hate is not so bad after all. It's all a matter of perspective, and by fighting the battles you may learn to love the things you thought you hated doing.

You might say, "I hate sales! Why would I want to learn about that?" or "I don't care about nutrition; I'll eat what I want." But note, it is estimated that about 80% of what you do on the way up your ladder are things you do not want to do.

There is no better example than the person who has never been to the gym and is fifty pounds overweight. When they begin their serious journey toward good health, the first three to six months are torturous. But as the battle goes on, the weight comes off, and that person gains confidence and feels better. Eventually, the tide turns; they wake up and can't wait to get to the gym.

How do I get started?

"Nothing in this world can take the place of persistence. Talent will not: nothing is more common than unsuccessful men with talent. Genius will not; unrewarded genius is almost a proverb. Education will not: the world is full of educated derelicts. Persistence and determination alone are omnipotent."

--Calvin Coolidge

Progressing through your 10,000-hour chosen area of expertise is a natural progression for most people because it is what we are raised to believe in and what society dictates. However, getting in your extra 1,000 hours in the other essential areas of success requires a specific, targeted effort.

The first thing that you will need to do is create the habit of continued learning. This means it becomes part of your daily routine or regiment. You can choose the time of day that works best for you. I personally do most of my continued learning while driving, listening to audible books, book summaries, podcasts, and short reels of my favorite mentors. I also make audio notes to myself of anything that has a personal positive impact on me. That's how I accumulated much of the content in this book.

When continued learning was first introduced to me, there were only two methods, reading books and attending seminars. Doesn't it seem astonishing how easy it is today, with all the technology and social media? Amazing content is easy to access, yet still less than 1% of us pursue improving ourselves and our future through continued learning. This is proof that ingrained habits of the past and social expectations inhibit most of us from pursuing a better life.

Take advantage of social media to follow people you admire. If I were speaking to a group of graduating high school students about this topic, I'd give them a list of 20 people to follow on Instagram. Anyone with a smartphone or a computer can do this. Watch 90-second reels by some of the greatest minds out there. Start with the mentors mentioned in this book. The education process is the first step to bringing yourself up to a new level of success. People get educated, read, listen, read more – but what's missing is the action. Eventually, you will act, and something good is going to happen.

Focus on a slow development of education, following the characteristics of successful people. It can take years and years – persistent improvement shows results eventually. These things need to be executed over a prolonged period of time. Changing the subconscious mind takes a LONG TIME. Watching people you admire every day programs your subconscious mind.

We may all respond to different types of inspiration. Look for positive content to propel your life further one day at a time so you can be a different person three and five years from now. Read one chapter or fifteen minutes a day. Get something that you are interested in or one or two mentors you really like. If you have bad behaviors or habits, after a couple months, you will find yourself thinking about what you read or learned. You start to question yourself. But if you don't read, those thoughts never cross your mind.

We are at a point in technology and history where, as long as you have a screen and an internet link, there is absolutely no excuse not to engage in continued learning.

- All highly successful people believe that if they do enough of the right things over a long enough period of time, they will have a good result
- All elite people share the characteristic of resilience – three weeks without results motivates them rather than driving them to quit. "If I want this and do this, eventually it is going to happen."

Forming a good habit

"First, we make a habit, and then our habits make us."
--John Dryden

It takes a minimum of at least 30 consecutive days to begin to change the subconscious mind to make a habit of auto-response. After 30 days of doing anything positive for yourself, you will start seeing results, feeling a sense of accomplishment. Then, the motivation to keep going kicks in.

So, for at least the first 30 days after you start your continued learning process, you must rely on discipline and know that you are going to fight a battle with yourself to execute this goal. Why do 95% or more New Year's resolutions go unfulfilled? Because of the lack of understanding that nothing changes in your mind in a day or a week. I'll state it again: a minimum of at least 30 days is required to begin to see results. Later in the book ,when we get into the actual ladder, you will clearly see that all high-level success takes time, and in most cases, a *lot* of time.

There are two books that are necessary for you to understand your habits and how to change them. *Atomic Habits* and *Change Your Habits, Change Your Life*. In fact, these would be excellent selections for you to launch your continued learning process with. If you're like me and don't like to read due to ADD issues, listen to audio books or get book summaries on Headway. Summaries are not the level of detail you will eventually need, but I want you to get started, and 15-minute summaries are a great avenue to begin with!

If you miss a day or get off track, you will use your daily ladder to wake up the next day and get right back on track. This will happen to you. It is imperative that you avoid the negative feedback loop: "I fucked up again, so just fuck it. I'm the same old me again."

This is the negative feedback loop we talked about, and it's an internal mental weakness that must be eliminated. Your new mentality will be "Damn, I fucked up today…but it's just one day, and I'm back on track tomorrow."

Almost everyone, when they commit to a new, good habit – quitting smoking, a diet, a promise to keep organized or keep up with a project - will mess it up within the first week. You should expect to make mistakes and have setbacks in any difficult endeavor. The trick is to get right back on the horse and start riding again every time.

Remember, motivation alone does not work. Repeat the actions and start over as many times as needed until the actions *become* motivation to stay on the horse for the ride of a lifetime. I promise you that by maintaining your discipline and resilience and fighting these daily battles, in just a few short months, you will be off to the races.

*"Discipline yourself to do the things you need to do when you need to do them, and **the day will come** when you will be able to do the things you want to do when you want to do them!"*
--Zig Ziglar

CHAPTER NINE

A MILLION-TO-ONE OR A MILLION-TO-NONE?

In a world full of copycats, be an original masterpiece!

You must be in the game!

As you have figured out by now, I view life as simply a game of odds and percentages. You have two choices in life: maximize your potential success by doing anything and everything possible to achieve your target, regardless of the odds, or embrace the feeling that it's too overwhelming or impossible –so why try?

All high-level successful people live in the million-to-one world. They have determination, passion, and unwavering belief in themselves. Those who live in the million-to-none mindset are committed to a self-inflicted, predetermined loss. Whether you make it or not, the effort you put into the million-to-one mindset will almost guarantee you an upward trajectory on your ladder. Everything you learn from the process of this mindset will transfer over positively to all aspects of your life. We will discuss a fixed mindset versus a growth mindset in preparation for the ladder chapter.

If you don't start, your chances are zero.

I have told you how the game of golf was a big part of my life, the change that launched me to every success I had since. My million-to-one lesson came via golf. I was a late bloomer to the game and did not even start playing until I was about 12 years old. Most elite athletes in any sport usually start much earlier, growing up with their chosen sport as part of their life and maybe even part of the family culture.

I did not come from an athletic family, and although my parents enjoyed professional sports, they did not push my brothers or me in that direction. Once I started playing, I was all in. I'd play every chance I got and found every opportunity to practice as much as I could. By the time I got to high school, I had become a pretty good junior player in the area, so I tried out and made the varsity high school team as a freshman. Since my home course was at the University of Maryland, I was exposed to the players on the University of Maryland team. It soon became my dream to one day play for the University of Maryland.

As my high school years continued, I improved not only in high school but in local tournaments as well. In fact, I never lost a high school match for three consecutive years, so I was feeling pretty good about my progress.

As is true in all sports and all aspects of life, moving up to the next level was a huge leap. My senior year, I realized that due to my late start, as well as some flaws in my game, I was nowhere near good enough to play for Maryland. After graduating, during the summer of 1978, I really put down the pedal with practice and playing times. I also spent time with the teaching pros at the club to improve my game.

Since I was not at a level for scholarship consideration by any schools, much less a Division 1 school like Maryland, I decided that I would try out for the team as a walk-on, even though I felt I had no chance to make the team. But what did I have to lose? I showed up.

We had both a fall and spring season, so the team tryouts were held at the beginning of the fall semester. At that time, I carried about a 2 handicap, which meant on a par 72 golf course, I was averaging about 74 shots per round. I knew going into the tryouts that the starting 6 players on the team had average scores below par.

The tryout was eight rounds, four at the home course and four at other quality courses in the area. The final roster for the team would consist of the top 12 finishers. Not only was my game statistically not good enough to make it, but the team was also returning five seniors from the previous year, all with exceptional talent and elite track records of performance. The coach had also had a good recruiting year, bringing in three more scholarship players to round out the incoming freshmen.

To say I was intimidated was an understatement. The only thing I had going for me was a good relationship with some of the elite players because this was my home club, and the coach was one of my instructors. So, in some ways, I at least felt like I had some people rooting for me to perform well.

The first round was at my home course, and it was a hot day in the mid-90s. This gave me some confidence, as I had always been an excellent hot-weather player. Most of my best rounds in my junior career came on days like that, so off I went. We played in threesomes, and I was paired with two incoming players that I did not know at all.

One of the deficiencies of my game was distance. This was back in the days of Persimmon wood drivers and steel shafts. The longest hitters could drive the ball 260 to 270 yards, a far cry from the 300-plus standard on the PGA tour today. My average driving distance was a meek 230 yards, which put me at significant disadvantage, especially when it came to reaching par 5s in two shots. However, I was a short game specialist, and my putting skills were exceptional.

When we teed off the first hole, there I was, 20 yards behind the other two guys, but I hit my second shot in there about 15 feet away, and birdied the first hole while the other players both made par. This was a huge relief of pressure and my confidence soared right away. I went on to shoot a round of even-par golf and was in the middle of the pack after day one. My excellent play continued for the next few rounds, and my confidence continued to grow.

When we got to the eighth and final round, I was tied with two other seniors for the last spot on the team. Up to that point, I had played by far my best consistent golf and was able to string the performance into several back-to-back rounds. At the same time, I wondered how this was happening. I also felt the pressure of the possibility that I might just pull this off.

The final round was at the home course, and again, it was a hot and humid day. I was paired with the two players I knew I had to beat to make the team. I also knew there were a few players only a few shots behind me. If one of them shot a low number, they could pass me up. Not only was this final round intimidating because of what was a stake, my direct competitors were both seniors. When you are an 18-year-old kid, a 23-year-old is a full-grown man. I had no idea what possessed me to perform like I did, but I birdied two of the first three holes while they were both 2 over par after three. I shot a final round 69 to qualify for the last place on the team, and the rest was history.

This experience changed me forever. I learned very clearly that, every now and then, you can defy the odds if you are in the game. My confidence soared, which motivated me to work even harder at my game. Remember that motivation is a result of deliberate actions.

The next year, I made the starting team and went on to be a full scholarship athlete, earning two varsity letters.

As we all know, this story could have gone very differently. Who knows? I might have needed to try again the next year. But the critical point to learn is that the more shots you take in life, the more likely one is going to land for you. Even if the odds are a million-to-one, the more often you show up to play with your best intentions and effort, the more likely you will eventually win a game. This philosophy transcends across all aspects of life. Show up often, and if it doesn't go your way, show up again, again, and again! Eventually, you will hit the grand slam in life.

When we are children growing up, virtually all of us persist in the million-to-one mindset. As time passes, and we start to understand the effort and grit it takes to succeed at anything worthwhile, we slowly slip into the million-to-none mindset: *I can't do it!*

How many 10-year-old boys lay in bed at night and dream of playing in the Major Leagues? They might have posters of their idol player in their room or may even have a book or two about baseball. They pretend it, imagine it, and wake up every day having dreamed about it. It does not occur to them that the actual chances of making it to the Major Leagues are worse than a million-to-one. Regardless of that, they wake up early to practice before school, hit the gym and work out the way their favorite player does, play on travel teams, and dream all day about the day they hit the winning home run in the World Series or pitch a no-hitter. Virtually nothing can distract the 10-year-old from his dream.

A 12-year-old girl who has discovered her talent for music and was gifted with an amazing voice lies in bed at night and dreams of being the next Taylor Swift and singing at a sold-out concert or maybe being on Broadway one day. She has posters of her favorite artist and routinely watches her favorite performers on social media. Again, the odds are less than a million-to-one, but what are her odds if she doesn't try? Someone makes it; it might as well be me!

These dreams are likely to fade as each of them is faced with stronger competition. They will likely find out that they are not the super talent they wished they were. This is where a critical part of who they will be the rest of their life comes into play. Do they step up their game, or do they listen to the ones telling them that they are not good enough?

I'm not saying that you increase your odds much by persisting when a coach or teacher tells you that you are not good enough. But what are your odds if you quit? Do you just accept that, or do you dig in and get to work twice as hard? Even the most talented humans only succeed with relentless drive and determination. If you quit with the first criticism or because of a negative coach, you will never know for the rest of your life what could have been.

Michael Jordan was cut from his high school basketball team. Kobe Bryant didn't score a point in his first season of elite ball at 14 years old. Tom Brady was not recruited out of high school and had no initial scholarship offers. Lady Gaga was bullied as a child and was told she could never make it because of her appearance.

If you love what you do and are good at it, maybe it's time to apply some resilience to work harder and smarter to improve your game. So, it's not whether you make it to the major leagues or sing on Broadway; it's whether you did everything you could have possibly done to make it happen. When you have exhausted every bit of effort, every obstacle, and every option, you can walk away, taking all the lessons, skills, and setbacks you learned in the process, and move on to the next phase of your life with a win. Concerted, disciplined, honest effort is never a failure! It always carries you to…next! Play the game even if it's a million-to-one.

The theory of chaos – within every disorder, there is order.

"Chaos was the law of nature; Order was the dream of man."
--Henry Adams

Related to the concept of a million-to-one or a million-to-none is the theory of chaos. It teaches us to expect the unexpected. By understanding that our ecosystems, our social systems, and our economic systems are interconnected, we can hope to avoid actions that may end up being detrimental to our long-term well-being.

According to the theory of chaos, everything has an order, regardless of how random, nonlinear, or unpredictable it may be. Every decision you make has extended infinite consequences that can be either positive or negative depending on the initial influence. This concept applies to micro decisions as small as what type of coffee you drink all the way to macro decisions like what college to attend.

Your ability to make consistent positive decisions from micro to macro in the spirit of living the Cheetah lifestyle will directly influence your long-term odds and percentages of climbing your ladder persistently. Of course, the opposite is true with a pattern of negative choices and decisions. Micro decision turbulence ensures that two adjacent points in a complex system will eventually end up in very different positions after some time has elapsed. Let's examine how this works in real life.

The Decision: leaving 10 minutes late.

Kate was yelling at her mom. "I'm late again for practice!"

Kate played on the junior varsity basketball team, and her coach had already spoken to her twice about being on time for practice. Kate's mom came running down the steps, yelling, "Hurry up and get in the car!"

The tension between the two was evident as Kate was frustrated that she was going to be late again. When quickly pulling out of the driveway, a neighbor noticed her aggressive driving and filed a complaint to the HOA, as several small children lived in the neighborhood. As they pulled out onto the main road, Kate told her mom to hurry up. Thus, Mom was pulled over for doing 50 in 35 mph zone.

Now Kate was going to be really late and was worried about the consequences. When she walked in, the coach said nothing but just let her fall into the drills that were being done. Kate was one of the star players on the JV squad and was a shoo-in for varsity the next year. At the end of practice, the coach reviewed the strategy for the next day's game and announced the starting lineups. Kate, who had started every game, was not on the list.

Again, the coach did not say a word to Kate. Kate had a ride home with a friend on the team, and when she walked in, she went to her room and slammed her door. Her mom tried to talk to her, but Kate was in no mood to speak her and called her a bitch.

All because she left 10 minutes late.

This is an example of the short-term theory of chaos. One event led to the next and the next and the next, all starting with one poor micro decision that started a string of negative events in both of their lives.

Fast forward to tryouts next year for varsity. The JV coach informed the varsity coach of the incoming players, and Kate was on the top of the list. The JV coach explained that she was talented and had a great work ethic and leadership skills, but was occasionally late. The varsity coach was a stickler for discipline and had no tolerance for being late.

Kate was only 6 months away from getting her license but still had to rely on her parents for transportation. Sure enough, Kate was late for two practices again, and she got cut from varsity to play another year on the JV team in spite of her great talent. Feeling totally dejected, Kate quit basketball. Her relationship with her mother deteriorated, and she started hanging out with the wrong crowd. All because a year earlier they left 10 minutes late. This is an example of the mid-term theory of chaos.

Over the summer of her sophomore year, Kate got her license and realized that now she could hold herself accountable. Her former teammates, now on the varsity team, explained to the coach that the situation was resolved. The varsity coach reached out to Kate and asked her to come to tryouts in the fall. Kate not only made the team but became an elite player in the county. She ditched the wrong crowd she had been hanging out with for her new friends and teammates. Kate went on to be a Division 1 scholarship athlete.

Kate vowed to never be like her mom and be responsible and accountable for her own success. She was the first one to practice and the last to leave. All of this was because of being 10 minutes late years earlier.

Kate's mom continued in her non-accountable victimized mode over the next 30 or 40 years, and always wondered why things just never went her way. It just seemed that the world was stacked against her. She lived a stressful life with strained relationships, especially with her children. This eventually led to guilt and regret. And it all started with being 10 minutes late. This is an example of the long-term theory of chaos.

This fictional story shows how one decision can lead to a pattern of despair while at the same time motivating someone else to recognize, "This is not the life for me."

Always remember the impact of your behavior and influence on others. In this story, Kate had an inner drive for something better, but it could have easily gone another way for her.

As you contemplate your future, who you are, and who you are going to be, it is imperative that you pay attention to all of your decisions and the micro-ones that may launch a pattern of negative successive outcomes for years moving forward. Of course, this works in reverse as well. Making positive, healthy decisions can launch you to the top tiers of your ladder. Making positive micro decisions is a habit based on your internal principles and following a pattern of ethical behavior. Basic reliability and accountability cannot be overstated when it comes to the theory of chaos and your outcomes in life. A winning lifestyle is a habit.

"Chaos is the score upon which reality is written."
-Henry Miller

CHAPTER TEN

THE ANDERSON EFFECT

"If you listen more than you speak, you will always say the right thing."
--Justin Freishtat

In the mid-1980s, I started my first business in the window treatment industry, selling blinds and shades out of the basement of the house I was renting. I was a one-man show, running sales leads during the week and installing the blinds on the weekends. Back in those days, the main avenues for marketing and lead generation were newspaper ads and Yellow Pages advertising. Leads were set by telephone with the use of an answering machine fielding the calls.

On one such lead, I went to an appointment in Northern Virginia to a new and high-value townhome. When I pulled up, there was a Black Jaguar XJS with chrome wheels in the driveway, which at the time was about the sexiest car on the market. Since I had always been a car guy, I knew right away that I would hit it off well with this prospect.

My knock was answered by a man in his late twenties, just a few years older than me. He looked like a cowboy in straight boot-cut jeans and cowboy boots. His voice had a charming drawl. I don't know exactly why, but his demeanor, along with the black Jag in the driveway, made me feel like I just met James Bond. This dude was a cool cat, and I was immediately drawn to find out more.

His name was Russell Anderson. After he bought one of my most expensive options for his living room, which were gold mirrored vertical blinds (yes, this was the 80s), I started asking questions about what he did for a living and his background. I just had a sense from his politeness and vivid personality that there was something special about this guy.

Sure enough, just as I suspected, he owned a chain of boot stores called Desperado's. He invited me to come to one of his boot stores to get a few pairs of boots and told me to make sure I contacted him personally so he could make sure he would take care of me on service and price. I had limited understanding of the value of relationships at that point in my business career, but due to my impression of this guy, I knew I had to go get me some boots. I met him at one of his locations and got my black panther snakeskin boots along with a traditional pair of brown cowhide boots. A few weeks later, I installed his blinds and thought that was the end of the story.

Moving ahead, two years later, my business was doing well, and I had just opened my second location in Northern Virginia. By total coincidence, I was at the store, which I only frequented about once a week to check in on my staff and have a weekly meeting, when who should walk through the door but Russell Anderson, the boot guy!

I immediately recognized him. He was the same guy I had met a few years earlier and still had the black Jag. He told me that he'd sold his boot stores to a partner and was now in the marketing and advertising business. He said he had some great ideas for my business and asked me to meet him for lunch to discuss his proposal. We set it up for the following week.

We had a great lunch, discussed my business in depth, and then came the magic sauce. He said, "Jerry, let me put some ideas for some ads together for you. I'll beta-test them for you at my expense, and if you like what you see and the results, we can talk about working together. What do you think?"

How do you say no to that? Up until this point in my sales and business career, I had never experienced anyone who was so confident in their ability to perform that they would do it for free to show me. This was an early lesson for me about bringing value to a relationship to build the relationship, and it transformed my entire business career. Russell's marketing efforts were exceptional, and we grew multiple businesses together for decades. We became best friends, and he became my life's mentor for not only business but my personal life as well. He introduced me to continued learning, and we frequently went to see the likes of Zig Ziglar, Brian Tracy, Tom Hopkins, and Denis Waitley.

We have now reached a 40-year friendship, a relationship based on loyalty and authenticity. Russell is one of the few truly authentic humans I have ever met, and his influence on me has been priceless.

You should note that if you value money over relationships, you will soon have neither.

> *"It's amazing what you can accomplish*
> *when you don't care who gets the credit."*
> --Harry S. Truman

The Best Year Yet

One of the most important principles I learned from Russell was what he called "The Best Year Yet."

Although I have used this in my businesses, when relating the performance of the business to my staff, it can certainly be applied to move up your ladder. The concept engages the principle of accumulation. At our new year annual meeting, we reviewed the performance of the previous year, then set our targets for the coming year.

By making each year better than the last, the accumulation of the efforts and results expands at a compounding rate.

This concept allowed me to expand our business operations and personal growth for seven consecutive years at my first business, five consecutive years at my second business, and sixteen consecutive years at my most recent business. If you are growing consistently in all aspects of your life on an annual basis, you are sure to be moving up your ladder on a consistent basis as well.

Russell also introduced me to the next level of sales. Although this is not a sales book, sales and negotiation will be a big part of your growth and success, even if you are not in sales as a profession. If you think about it, all relationships require sales and negotiating skills. How you deal with your employer, spouse, children…or even getting a date or being socially active all require sales and negotiating skills. Talented people in the sales negotiation arena generally live a better personal life simply due to the knowledge that they are in more control. People proficient in sales and negotiation are more confident in their daily lives, which leads to a higher level of attractiveness.

As I mentioned earlier in relation to long-term growth, an education in the sales arena and putting in your 1,000 hours is essential to your long-term success.

Although I learned all the old-school sales methods from the experts like Tom Hopkins, Zig Ziglar, and Brian Tracy, who taught the sales skills of tie downs, presentation skills, handling objections, and closing, the most valuable sales skills I learned from my lunch meeting with Russell.

What value can I bring to my prospect, and what problem can I solve for them?

I like to refer to salespeople as either salesmen or sales professionals. A salesman is focused on himself and bringing in a sale today. A salesman has that old stigma of the 1970s used car sales guy.

On the other hand, a sales professional focuses on the relationship and solving problems. The sales professional believes 100% in the product and has an authentic interest in prospects, which establishes a quality reputation. This leads to the golden goose, which is an endless feed of referrals. The prospect feels empowered and comfortable in their decision to do business with you. There is never buyer's remorse.

I taught my sales staff to always be *sales professionals*. I wanted them to *be* the conversation. I did not want my customers to say what an amazing company or they loved our products. I wanted them to discuss the relationship they had with my representative. We preached this concept to anyone who had contact with a client, from customer care to our delivery drivers. Authenticity, along with accountability, in your sales staff is the path to 5-star reviews and a business that is unbreakable! Of course, you must have the back-end infrastructure of exceptional service and quality controls in place as well. If you are a young aspiring sales professional, make sure you are aligned with a company that engages in these philosophies.

This same approach works in personal relationships as well. Try it, and you will see your world open to endless possibilities. If you live your life as one of providing value and expecting nothing in return, everything you ever wanted will come your way.

> *"You can have everything in life you want if you*
> *will just help other people get what they want."*
> --Zig Ziglar

CHAPTER ELEVEN

THE FUNK FACTOR

If you can't outplay them, outwork them.
--Ben Hogan

When you hear someone say, "You will not outwork me," you are most likely speaking with a Cheetah. It's a mindset committed to routine and regiment. Having an excellent work ethic is more than just doing the hard work. Don't get me wrong here, working hard under any circumstances is better than being a Sloth. A Sloth aims at nothing and hits it every time. It's important to think about *how* you do the hard work, too. We have all heard that saying, "Work smarter, not harder," but the reality is that working harder makes you smarter. If you are looking to avoid the work in the climb, save yourself the effort and be a happy Sheep.

Keep these considerations in mind when it comes to effort:
What am I learning?
Am I learning correctly?
Do I have the right coach?
How am I growing in the process while busting my ass?
Is my work evolving?
Are others benefiting from my efforts?
Am I benefiting from my efforts?

Be aware of the quality of your work, not just the quantity. If an athlete is practicing a new mechanic for muscle memory but is practicing the movement wrong, they are actually and unknowingly ingraining a bad habit. The longer we develop a process the wrong way, the more difficult it is to correct it later.

Although it may be more difficult up front, always try to learn things the right way early in your journey so you can execute with excellence.

Take pride in how you perform. Leave people your best work. I like to call this "putting your signature on it." Remember, we collect wins daily. When you know you gave something your best effort, it feels damn good, right?

"The magic you're looking for is in the work you are avoiding."
--Dipen Parmar

Fred Funk: legendary work ethic

"You have to work hardest for the things you want the most."
- Carol Dweck

When I was a freshman at the University of Maryland, one of the seniors on my golf team was a kid named Fred Funk. I knew Fred from years of hanging around the course because, like me, he was a local kid. Fred had an outgoing personality and was always willing to invite me to play a round or two with him.

After Fred graduated from Maryland, he turned pro and became the golf coach. In fact, he was my coach during my senior year. Fred was small in stature at 5' 8" and weighed maybe 160 pounds, but he had a Lion's heart. I identified well with him since we were both short hitters who relied on our short game play. We came from similar backgrounds and childhoods where we had to work for anything we wanted. Like me, Fred was always working side jobs to make money to support himself. We both also juggled work, full-time school, and playing a full-time varsity sport.

When in his mid-twenties, while working as a pro at the club and being the golf coach, Fred went to work with relentless effort on his golf game.

I'll never forget a night in the summer of 1978, the year I graduated from high school. I pulled into the driving range parking lot at 11:45 at night with my girlfriend (our go-to place). I couldn't believe my eyes: I saw someone hitting balls out of the bunker at the end of the driving range. The range closed at 10:00, but since we were required to clean up and pick up all the balls, making things ready for the morning shift, the range lights stayed on until midnight.

As I walked closer to see what idiot was practicing on a Friday night at 11:45pm, I recognized Fred. I was there with my girlfriend after a night of drinking and partying, and Fred was practicing his golf game.

Hmm, can we learn something here?

Fred's father used to do some work for me, installing window shades at my first company, and on one occasion I went by his house to drop off some supplies. Fred was in the backyard, swinging a wisp broom. Bemused, I asked Fred, "What the hell are you doing?"

He explained, "The resistance of the broom creates a better rhythmic swing."

"How often do you do this?" I exclaimed.

"An hour every day," answered Fred. Remember, this was long before video and golf-swing training aids. What's one of the characteristics of an Alpha Lion? *Innovation.* Lesson learned.

Over the next few years, Fred began to dominate the Mid-Atlantic local professional tournaments. He was an amazing bad-weather player and dominated in those conditions, whether it was rain, wind, or cold.

He won the Mid-Atlantic Open by shooting a course record on the final day in horrific conditions: a windy, rainy day with temperatures in the upper 40s. This was nothing short of amazing. I and everyone else knew there was something special going on with Fred.

Let me take you back to Sunday, May 3, 1992, to the Shell Houston Open at the Woodlands in Texas. Fred's PGA professional career was well entrenched at this point, but that elusive victory had escaped him like most professionals in their pursuit of ultimate glory. A win on the PGA tour is not only a rare occurrence but also reserved for only the most elite of the elite. It takes Alpha Lion characteristics to even come close to approaching this level of success. Coming off Saturday's course shooting a record-breaking 62, Fred found himself on the 18th hole with a two-shot lead and one more swing away from the victory. Standing 175 yards away from the pin, Fred simply needed to be conservative and hit a shot to the middle of the green, which would allow him to take up to 3 putts and still win the tournament. The issue was the entire flight was over water, and any mishap, error in calculation, or mental hiccup entering into the mix would put his shot in the water. The next golf swing would be a legacy moment. It would be the culmination of 20 years of blood, sweat, and tears, all concentrated in one moment. Was the effort worthy of the result? Were the thousands of hours of practice enough? Was the inner belief in himself unwavering? When preparing for a moment like this in life, the moment was already predetermined by the history of the effort, by the work ethic that only a few know about, the mental and physical preparation, and a vision of executing this situation thousands of times in your mind. Does the pressure elevate you to excellence or crush you to failure?

I was watching this unfold on TV by myself, and like everyone else, the nerves of the situation were overwhelming. Was the underdog actually going to pull this off? I thought. Then I was reminded of the resiliency of the Fred I knew from childhood and told myself, of course, he is! One of the most important factors in executing under pressure is routine. Do the same exact routine, whether it's a practice shot on the driving range or a 175-yard 6 iron to win a PGA tour event.

The pin was tucked on the front right of the green, close to where the ball would have to travel the longest distance to clear the water. Fred had been shooting at pins all day as his game was performing to perfection. However, this called for a conservative shot left and long of the flag. As Fred approached his set up to the ball, he looked up at the green and backed away. He set up again and backed away again. I was immediately concerned because this was definitely a break in routine. Fred told me later that he could not get comfortably lined up for the shot he wanted to hit. As Fred stepped in for the third time, he took his usual compact swing, but I could tell, even on TV, that it was not his normal balanced swing of perfection. I started to panic as we all stood and waited to see if the ball was going to clear the water. The ball hit the front bank and cleared the water by a few feet. The rough around the lake held the ball in play, and Fred was a chip and putt away from history. Fred won his first PGA tour event!

Although it wasn't perfect, I want you to clearly understand that the diligent lifelong effort was enough to execute under the most trying circumstances. If the effort over a lengthy duration was not enough, the conclusion to this story would have been quite different. The victory started 20 years earlier!

As you will hear a few different times in this book, "You do not live in the moment…you live for the moment," and this was Fred's moment of glory that led to lifetime of exceptionalism. It was preceded by a lifetime of diligent work, relentless effort, and an unwavering deep-seated belief that this day would come.

Just like Eminem said in *8 Mile*:

> *"Look, if you had one shot, one opportunity*
> *To seize everything you ever wanted- One moment*
> *Would you capture it or just let it slip?"*

Fred Funk went on to an incredible PGA Tour and Senior PGA Tour Career. He had 29 professional wins, eight of which were on the PGA Tour, including winning The Players Championship in 2005, as well as the US Senior Open. He became a decamillionaire, landing several sponsorships and commercials along the way. Well into his 50s, he was still playing PGA Tour events.

How was this possible for a guy with average natural talent, few resources, and no financial backing? The relentless pursuit can never be measured by anyone except the person who is engaged in it. In fact, we both played with some elite, talented players, a few of whom seemed destined to be on the PGA tour...but none of them made it except Fred.

Let's look at this in more depth.

I had the good fortune to caddy for Fred in his first two PGA tour events. I was a junior at Maryland and 22 years old at this time.

I was an adequate amateur player by this time, and my game had developed nicely over the past few years. But when I saw what the PGA tour was all about and how good the players were, I faced one of my life's biggest crossroads. Should I double-down my efforts and commitments or quit my dreams? I decided to take the path of least resistance at that time in my life, and I quit!

I'm sure that during the process of Fred's path to the PGA tour, he faced crossroads multiple times. Each and every time, he chose the hard route: more work, more dedication, finding a way. There was no quit in Fred, and his resilience was unshakeable. I can also tell you firsthand that he must have had a resilient inner belief in himself that was "all in"

- because no one else thought he had what it took! None of us could ever imagine what he was destined for.

For those of us who quit too soon, well, we live with the "What if?" forever. When do you know it's time to move on? Either your dream changes, or after you have exhausted all options, and you can truly say to yourself, "I gave it my very best, and it wasn't good enough." Either way, the work ethic you poured into the effort will always be an integral part of your inner makeup and can be applied to other goals and dreams for the rest of your life moving forward. The experiences and results of any worthy effort toward a dream or goal will firm up your foundation for what's next.

The pandemic parable

"Perform without purpose so you are ready for the moment!"
--David Goggins

Once you develop a reputation for unwavering work ethic, you gain a level of respect from your peers or employees. I always believed in leading by example while letting others see my efforts. This has always served me well in the business world. What happened to my business during the COVID-19 outbreak is a prime example of this.

When COVID-19 hit the world in the spring of 2020, I had just turned 60 years old. I still had the same bounce in my step and spark in my mind as when I was a young man. I attribute this mostly to my focus on what I call extreme health and my amateur career in bodybuilding.

Little did I know what a benefit this would be in the coming months. My company was in the home food delivery business, and we were doing about $8 million in annual sales at that time. Our focus was on customization and bulk delivery of high-end healthy proteins. We were known for impeccable quality, quick delivery, and exceptional customer care.

March 8, 2020, was the day my world changed. The government shut down schools and implemented an essential-service-only policy for businesses to be open. Due to our large customer base and stellar reputation, our inbound inquiries increased ten times overnight. I immediately called in my management staff to strategize not only how to oversee the mass influx of orders but how we would fill and deliver those orders. I was very fortunate to have a group of exceptional people completely dedicated to the mission, our customers, and to each other.

None of us knew the intensity of the storm that would come in the next few days. As the appointment flow for our service kept building, we pivoted on several fronts to keep up with the seemingly impossible task. For example, we were an in-home sale, but COVID-19 prevented us from entering people's homes, so we quickly transitioned to a virtual Zoom sale. My tech team put together a Zoom presentation and an electronic contract within 24 hours. I was on the phone with all our suppliers, tripling inventory orders and setting up systems with them to handle the volume. The sales team began doing Zoom presentations with sales at a rate of up to 10 a day per salesperson, whereas previously, our reps visited one or two homes per evening per representative.

As the orders came in, we did not have the capacity to fill and pack the orders or get them all delivered. Several of our staff had high school kids that came to work for us, since schools were closed. We trained them all in 48 hours and put them to work in our freezers and delivery trucks. We did not have enough trucks or drivers to keep up the quick delivery service we normally provided. I knew that if I could figure out how to keep the quick delivery and service levels, this could launch our company's growth to an exponential level.

One of our main suppliers delivered to restaurants. However, since restaurants were closed, I worked out a deal with them to keep some of their drivers employed and to use a few of their refrigerated trucks. We paid staff double-time to work on Sundays and allowed the drivers to work as many hours as they preferred. There was nothing I would not do to assist in this process to keep our company performing and doing a stellar job for our customers.

Throughout this six-month surge in our business, my staff saw me in the trenches. For the first three months, I worked 18 to 20 hours a day, seven days a week. No one knew that I stayed to pack orders myself until 2am or delivered emergency orders to people on Sunday mornings, but the staff knew I was fully engaged with them every step of the way. This is leading by example. It was the relentless work ethic required for any small entrepreneurial business.

When you say, "I'll do whatever it takes," do you mean it? Do you have the resilience to battle through? That six-month all-encompassing battle enabled me to double the size of my company and sell to a private equity investor for a substantial sum.

Keep the long-term vision going in the tough times and while in the trenches. Good things come to those who endure!

The previous 19 years of work, grind, and experience prepared me for "the moment." Our company systems, staff, vendor relationships, and reputation, built over those 19 years, were the pillars of our execution. It is imperative as you move up your ladder that your thought process is always preparing for "the moment." You will never know when it will come - but faith in the fact that *it will come* is a Cheetah belief. If I do enough of the right things long enough and often enough, great things are going to happen! **You do not live in the moment; you live *for* the moment.**

CHAPTER TWELVE

SEEK RISK...CONQUER FEAR

"He who seeks risks creates security;
he who seeks security risks everything."
- Denis Waitley

Fear is simply the misuse of your imagination.

The fears we create

If I asked, "Are you satisfied with where you are, what you have, and all your expectations in life?" not a single person would answer yes to that question. The reason is simple. Humans are built to achieve, which means that we have a relentless inner yearning to be more than what we are.

However, inner fears and insecurities guide us instead down the "safe" path. Most people don't live; they simply exist. The traditional perceived safe path will only get you so far, and your ladder will try to set your ceiling far below your potential. Don't be afraid that something will happen, be afraid that nothing will happen!

In this chapter, we will examine the counterintuitive nature of risk. As you attain new heights on your ladder as a Cheetah, you'll experience heightened levels of uncertainty. Scary, yes! Yet facing your fears and taking risks *is* the safe path. Following the path of least resistance or the perceived safe path will simply loop you right back to where you started with exactly what you started with. This path to nowhere is where the

Sheep roam forever in a world of complacency. Success will never fall in your lap; you must go get it, and that pursuit requires risk. Seeking risk means constantly challenging yourself to new heights.

By taking risks, you will enhance your learning opportunities, increase motivation, have valuable experiences, overcome fears, build confidence, and, of course, reap the financial rewards. These are all of the essential characteristics of living an exceptional life.

More than 90% of what we fear is simply the misuse of our imagination. Most of you are familiar with Metallica's legendary song "Enter Sandman," where they describe the irrational fears of children related to the dark. The song was also used when the legendary baseball closing pitcher for the New York Yankees, Mariano Riveria, came into the game to send all the batters to never, never land. As children, we all feared monsters under our bed or ghosts in the closet. As I am sure you remember, this picture in your imagination was the very embodiment of terror. A sprint down to Mom and Dad's room was a sure source of relief when you convinced yourself that your fear was real and that monster was going to get you.

As adults, we may no longer fear a nebulous monster in the closet, but we continue to worry, misconstrue, and act based on our irrational fears. The difference now versus your childhood is that we don't have a resource to make us feel better, so we internalize the fear. We allow that fear to keep us from taking necessary actions to propel us forward to the world we expect to live and thrive in. The longer you let these irrational fears engulf your mind, the more likely that you will choose a life of safety and security that will land you 50 years from now exactly where you are today. This is why a Sheep will almost certainly be doomed to a life of regret.

Of course, this relates to the million-to-one mindset. If you look at life through the lens of odds and percentages, it will help you battle through many of your fears. The odds of being killed in a plane crash are about one in 11 million, so get on that plane, no matter how uncomfortable you are.

Remember, all success comes from an uncomfortable place. Get used to it. Learn what it feels like. Make it part of your inner culture. View it as a challenge, and yes, reward yourself when conquering something that required you to get uncomfortable and overcome fear. The more you challenge yourself, the more habits will form. Eventually you will get comfortable with being uncomfortable in facing your fears.

I want you to remember that your insecurities about any fear or challenge are perfectly normal. We all have them, so stop beating yourself up and thinking, "Why am I like this? No one else is!" Wrong! The question is, will you accept those insecurities and fears like a Sheep, or will you engage in risk like a Cheetah and conquer those fears over time?

We have little control over our initial, instinctive thought or fear – what you might call the "gut" or "knee-jerk" reaction…but we get to choose our next thought. Every time you take a risk related to a fear, you are one more rung up your ladder, regardless of the outcome. The action of "going for it" alone moves you to a better path.

I have used several methods to address fears. Most come in the form of a question to myself.

- What's the worst thing that can happen?
- Is this going to kill me?
- And my favorite, what's the alternative? Asking this question puts you in a place to assess what you have now, which will remain unchanged if you do not act. "If I do nothing, I'll still have what I got now. Is that the outcome I want?" Eventually, this mindset will get you wins, and as wins accumulate, so will you.

There is no magic to taking on more risk. Have you ever wondered why the Nike logo is so simple: "Just do it." It's because life really is that simple, but we complicate it by overthinking. If you want it…do it, period!

Be ready today

My second oldest son is kind of my prodigy. He was the risk taker and daredevil of the family. If there had been X Games and BMX racing when I was a kid, I assure you that I would have been deeply engaged in those activities. All I had was my Schwinn Sting Ray, and yes, we were best friends. There was nothing we would not try together. There were many trips to the emergency room.

My son became very proficient in skateboarding and BMX riding in his mid-teens when he took the leap to the dirt bike world in Moto X. We took a few tours around to some local tracks where he perfected his short jumping skills and speed. I said, "What the hell!" and got on a bike myself only to end up with a cracked rib and sprained ankle, so I was out of the game quickly…just too old to take the beating.

My son asked me to take him to one of the larger tracks with bigger and longer jumps. When we arrived, an ambulance was in the parking lot, and I asked who got hurt, and he replied, "No one…yet."

In front of us was a larger course with a jump of about 80 feet.

My son said, "I'm doing that today."

I asked, "How? Aren't you afraid?"

He replied, "Yes, but I'm ready. I've been preparing for this for about a year."

I was terrified, but as a parent, I knew this was his moment, and I would not take it away from him. Instead, I told the ambulance attendant to be on standby.

After about 30 minutes of measuring up the jump and getting a feel for the speed and distance, off he went. I knew right away from the launch he overshot the landing area, so he landed hard on the front tire, which threw him up off the bike toward the handlebars, but he gained control and landed it.

This is a simple story of preparation, calculation, and having worked long and hard enough to have the confidence to execute. He had his moment of glory, and isn't that what life is all about? His abilities in the arena of extreme sports built his confidence growing up and led to the quality man he is today. Remember, parents, what matters most is that your kids feel good about themselves and build confidence growing up. The number one skill of successful kids is hopefulness. Encourage your kids to be hopeful, take calculated risks, and do what they are good at.

The remedy of preparation

"I have learned that success is to be measured not so much by the position that one has reached in life as by the obstacles which he has overcome while trying to succeed."
--Booker T. Washington

Your biggest fear in life should be being *unprepared*. The good news is, this fear is in our complete control. Do the work!

Many times, you can reduce fear with preparation. Public speaking is one of life's greatest fears. However, through preparation, you can reduce the fear. As the motto goes, "Don't practice getting it right; practice so you can't get it wrong." Whatever the task at hand, practice, rehearse, repeat until you are overprepared. There it is again: hard work, pain, and suffering. I keep telling you that this is at the core of all high-level success. Are you on board yet?

Of course, taking on risk does require some calculation. There is a line to walk, the energetic zone between being risk-averse and being simply reckless. Learn to be a risk-seeker. Over the years, you will endure some losses, but your wins will signifyingly overshadow them. I had the privilege to lose a million or more three different times in my life. I say privilege because I had previously taken the risk, so I had those millions to lose. I was successful enough to where this kind of "loss" could occur, and because I had done it before, I could do it again. Each time, the recovery outshined the loss. If I were risk averse, I never would have made the millions to begin with. More importantly, I stayed risk-focused each time I endured a loss to build my empire back better than it was before.

The same concept holds true in relationships. Many of us choose the wrong spouse early in life and end up as a divorce statistic. Again, you can become risk averse with a victim mentality, saying, "I'm never doing that again!" Or, you can learn from the first mistake, take a risk by putting yourself back out there, and you may find the person put on this Earth for you. That's exactly what happened to me!

Seeking a risk-free, complacent, conforming lifestyle will not move you up the ladder. There is no neutral gear in life. When you are not growing, by default, you are shrinking. Without growth your ladder will begin to tilt downward and year after year the pain of regret will grow!

I urge you to take significant risks while you are young. The benefits are immeasurable, and the losses are more easily eradicated. In youth, you not only have more time to rebuild but your responsibilities and commitments are fewer.

Here are a couple of examples of this practice, successfully navigated by people who mean the world to me:

My son took a year off between high school and college to play hockey full-time to see if he could elevate his game to get noticed by D1 or professional scouts. That did not work out, so off to college he went. Yes, he was a year behind, but the risk was limited due to his age and no other obligations.

On the other hand, my father took all of his savings and went into debt to buy a small business when he was in his mid-thirties. This might not seem terribly risky, but add in a mortgage, three young children, and little business experience, and this risk starts to seem more reckless.

But my parents, who had struggled financially their entire lives, had a different vision for our family, so *not* buying the business was the real risk. They were committed to a better life.

The business was a small retail store where my dad *built relationships* with the other nearby entrepreneurs. A few more rungs up the ladder got him educated in finance and investing. They went on to be 30-year business owners who retired millionaires. To this day, my respect for their risk tolerance, given the circumstances, is inspiring.

When I asked my dad about the decision and the related risk, he simply replied, "What was the alternative?"

It was a great lesson for myself and my two brothers, who all went on to be successful entrepreneurs.

Seeking risk is the evolution of constantly challenging yourself to new heights. If you pay now you will play later…if you play now you will pay later…seek safety in risk!

CHAPTER THIRTEEN

VICTIM OR VICTOR

In life, the comeback is always greater than the setback. Find those who have been in the trenches, who suffered difficult times, who may have lost everything only to rebound to new heights on their ladder. I have never met anyone who has achieved anything worthwhile who didn't at some point recover from an event that caused severe pain and suffering.

It's all part of the game.

"Nothing important comes easy. Pain, discomfort, and disruption are necessary counterparts to growth and change."
--Dr. Brad Sachs

When we go through something so emotionally traumatic and draining it is easy to think of all the ways in which we felt slighted, injured, deceived, or betrayed. However, remember my attitude about taking the "easy" path: it won't get you very many rungs up your ladder. Blaming someone else and dwelling on the past is the victim's path. Yes, even if you were the one wronged. There is no benefit to being the victim. Victors refuse to entertain self-pity and excuses; they learn and move on. Understand this up front: No one is going to cry for you. They have their own tears.

When facing any adversity, we have two choices: deny and justify, or accept and correct. Option one is the easy path; option two is more difficult. As you know by now, successful outcomes in life require the difficult path. When you repeatedly take the difficult path, you prove to yourself and your subconscious that this is the path to glory.

The "deny and justify" path is ingrained in our subconscious minds because that is what we do to ease the pain in the short run. We blame someone or something else. "There is no way I caused this."

"Accept and correct" requires full accountability, assessment, evaluation, and change.

You may become victim to many unexplained outside circumstances, sometimes having nothing to do with your direct actions. Even in these situations the winners in life are in learning mode to quickly reverse the victimization to a victor mind set. *Circumstance does not change responsibility!* Within all darkness lies a rainbow.

In this chapter, I will share with you my life changing journey from "deny and justify" to "accept and correct" as I talk about my divorce from my first wife. There are few things in the human experience that can be as grueling as a divorce – especially when there are children involved. And, as is always the case, there are two sides to every story. Stay tuned.

Understanding "fairness" in life

> *"Most of us end up in quiet desperation."*
> – Joe Rogan

Many people let the world dictate their destiny. They have an inherent belief: "No matter what I do, the world is unfair. It's just a matter of time until it's my turn to have negativity – or even tragedy -thrust upon me."

So let me ask you this question. If you know life is unfair, is it unfair? I really want you to think about that question because we are getting to the core of the difference between the Sheep and the Cheetahs. If you really think about it, and you know upfront that life is unfair, then there can be nothing unfair about it. You see, when you take 100% accountability for everything – and by everything, I mean those things in your control and those things out of your control – you will be a victor in life because you will never see yourself as a victim to an external event or situation.

This is a difficult concept for many to grasp. You must believe that luck is self-created. We have all heard the phrase "the harder I work, the luckier I get," which, in its true explanation, means that we manifest our own luck and therefore control our destiny. We have also heard the phrase, "Everything he touches just seems to turn to gold." Again, this is an individual who has an embedded "victor" mindset that, through years of regimented commitment and self-belief, executes consistently to produce winning results.

I am amazed how many people labor under the belief that their past circumstances and life events define their future. Sadly, in many cases, this belief excuses someone to be a "victim" for the rest of their life. This mentality leads to a miserable existence. The most common victim thought is the blame game: It was my parents, it was my divorce, a tragic loss, it's how I look, it's my insecurity or lack of intelligence, and the list goes on.

Well, I hate to simplify it this much, but common sense always prevails. What does your past have to do with today, tomorrow, and the rest of your life? So many people fall victim to their past and their experiences and hold an inner belief that the past defines not only who they are but their destiny in life. Nothing could be further from the truth. Anyone can start to climb a different ladder and a different life as of this minute! It's a simple decision, but you will need to want to make it.

So far, you have not heard the easy route promoted anywhere in this book, and you won't. We discussed at length the battle required for all worthwhile achievement. This battle is no different. If you want to win and live a victor lifestyle, the battle to that outcome is a long, hard, difficult one.

Whenever faced with a difficult decision, a challenge or any type of controversy or a discipline issue, that requires any type of action I ask myself, "**What's the alternative?**"

I have this question in front of me everywhere: on sticky notes in my car, next to my bed, and at my desk. It's my way of holding myself accountable to never fall into a victim mindset again. I'm always thinking, "If I don't do this, I will get this."

If you, like many, have some aspect of the victim mentality haunting you, use this question as a launching pad. You know what you have now. You know how you feel as a victim. Why not start the process of holding yourself accountable? It's you, not them! Catch your negative victim thoughts and immediately go to this question. It's a long way up the ladder, but this will start you on the path one rung up at a time.

The victim is in a comfortable place strolling down the easy path in life and feeling sorry for themselves. The victim looks for an outside source or someone else to be the villain; it removes all responsibility and accountability. They leech onto other people, are compulsive complainers, and are overall unhappy, miserable people with little self-esteem. I was one of them.

Just look at the billion-dollar psychology industry where everyone runs to for solutions. My approach to relinquishing the victim villain that is parked in your brain is simply taking new actions.

First, you must remove all relationships that are reinforcing your victimization. And yes, I mean anyone, including family and friends. Do not be afraid of being alone. Sometimes, this is where you will rediscover the real you.

Second, get busy and do something different. Like everything else related to success in life, it begins with that first step. Leave that job you hate, start dating again, do some volunteer work, move to a new city. Put yourself in a place to meet new people and build new relationships. Any new actions will start the process.

Third, flood yourself with positive information daily, whether through social media or reading and listening to self-education books. This learning process is the beginning of changing your subconscious mind.

Most importantly join a gym, hire a trainer, and launch a new healthy lifestyle. You will be amazed at how quickly the outlook changes.

Take the first step! Again, like the Nike logo—Just do it!

> *"99% of people let others' opinions and beliefs*
> *keep them from ever living the life they want."*
> *--Andy Frisella*

The Reliant Life

> *"We are not victims of our situations. We are the architects of it."*
> --Simon Sinek

I carried this victim mentality to various degrees until I was 40 years old, when the most tragic event in my life turned into the best thing that ever happened to me.

As I mentioned earlier, when I was a child and as a young man, I had a burning desire to get the things I wanted. I discovered early that by latching on to people who gave me the avenue to my end result, I was very successful in achieving my goals and desires. This wouldn't seem out of the ordinary, as we all gain from building relationships. However, what I did was a little different. I was in it for me and me only. Any value I provided to the other side of the relationship was exclusively based on what the relationship was bringing me. As soon as any of these relationships could not provide what was in it for me, I was gone.

In some ways this made me what I call an unintentional Snake. A Snake that negatively affected other people without intending to do so. Why I exhibited this subconscious behavior I developed in my childhood I could not exactly explain.

And guess what? Not only does it not matter, I also don't care. We all have unexplained bullshit that we grew up with, and it's irrelevant to the long-term accountability as an adult in your life. You don't need to know why; you just need to know what you are going to do about it. In spite of this unknowing detrimental behavior, I was a young man with a big heart and full of kindness. Sounds conflicted? Yes.

Over the years, I became an expert in this course of behavior, and it led to what I call a reliant life. That was a life where my personal success was, in my mind, attributed to others who I thought were more intelligent than me. I relied exclusively on others for my personal success due to my lack of self-esteem and lack of confidence. Because I was somewhat of a flamboyant personality and had an incredible work ethic, I portrayed the exact opposite of who I was inside. Those characteristics served me well as I journeyed through what I thought was great personal success. When you seek success through other people, the law of attraction works in reverse. You will tend to attract people into your life who are drawn to you for the wrong reasons.

There were endless examples of how my reliant life had negative impacts on my relationships but the two of the biggest decisions I made from this mindset in life would later come back to haunt me tremendously. I lived this reliant lifestyle until I was 40 years old, when my world shockingly changed.

In the 1980s, my brother and I ran extremely successful businesses in the window treatment industry (blinds and shades). My brother was on the manufacturing side, while I was in the retail side of the business.

When the 1990 recession struck, my brother sold his manufacturing operation to a large conglomerate, and my business took a dip due to market conditions. One day, we talked about setting up a new model, where we would manufacture direct to retail. My brother was super sharp with systems, technology, and finance, and I was well versed in sales, marketing, and operations. Although I could outwork anyone, I always viewed my brother as the intelligent one in the family.

So naturally, when this opportunity came along, I thought that he was the one to take me to the neverland of millions. Just like the same flawed behavior from the past, I latched onto him for my personal benefit. I did the grunt work and enjoyed the ride to stardom that he created.

We were an amazing team at first, and the business thrived from day one. In four short years, we built a $20 million operation with 60 employees, 18 retail stores, and a large in-home sales team. You would think all was heavenly, but our relationship began to deteriorate. As the company grew, we disagreed on the direction of the company and many decisions on the growth strategy. I was stuck in a small-company mindset, and he was building systems for a much larger operation.

My lack of flexibility and understanding of the growth process led to the demise of our relationship. I did not understand that there was more than one way to skin the cat. He saw clearly that I had become a detriment to the growth and culture of the company, and we parted ways in an ugly departure where he ended up buying out my 50% of the company.

Why did all of this happen? Again, I could not get what I wanted from the relationship anymore, so I put myself in a position to fail. The same pattern continued!

Whether I admitted it to myself or not, I had tremendous regret for putting money in front of my relationship with my brother, and the whole process left me feeling guilty and empty inside. I lost a big part of my dignity, and to complicate things even more, I had nothing on the horizon to look forward to professionally. I distinctly remember thinking once I got those millions, I had made it life. Little did I know it was the beginning of the end!

There is an old saying about money that goes, "If you didn't earn it, you burn it." It's not that I didn't actually earn it through hard work, but it was how the money was acquired on bad terms that made me feel unworthy of the apparent success.

In an epilogue to these difficult experiences, you all should know that my brother and I did not speak to one another for a few years. But thankfully, slowly, we reconciled our relationship. After I took full accountability for my role in the demise in concise communication with him, we now have a clear understanding of each other and a normal family relationship. It was no surprise to me that he went on to build an operation that was close to $100 million in sales!

To hell and back

"When you are no longer able to change a situation…
you are challenged to change yourself."
--Victor Frankel

Not everything in life can be fixed. Sometimes, you just need to walk away.

The most important decision of your life is the person you choose for your life partner. When I married my first wife at the age of 25, it was exclusively based on the premise outlined above. She was a smart, beautiful, talented lady whom I perceived as strong and confident. I was attracted to her as someone who would make life easier for me, as she would be the one to steer the ship and take care of things.

At the time, it never crossed my mind that we were not aligned on all of the important things that a person should consider when taking on a life partner. We had vastly different cultural backgrounds, different values, different dreams, goals, and visions. I was a high-risk taker; she was an ultra-conservative personality. I thought I was going to mold her into my world, and she was looking to escape hers. Subconsciously, I discarded all logic against our union because the power of "what's in it for me" again overshadowed all logical thinking. Every great relationship starts with "what's in it for us!" At that point in my life, I had no understanding of that concept. We were doomed from the start, and I bet she would tell you the same thing. After 13 years and four children, things ended badly.

After our fourth child was born and we became wealthy from the sale of my share of the company to my brother, things were never the same. I carried guilt and regret inside me. My wife was unhappy as our worlds did not align. Our relationship deteriorated over the next few years.

We tried all the usual remedies: marriage counseling, books, and friends' advice. The efforts I put forth seemed met with a wall of resistance. Something was wrong, but I just figured it was a rough patch. We would battle our way through the same way I approached everything else in life. I was convinced that I was responsible for whatever problems we had.

Eventually, my wife asked me to move out for a month or two, as she needed some time to contemplate our relationship and the future. Telling the kids was heartbreaking. I took full accountability for the situation in that conversation. Thinking this was a short-term arrangement, I moved into my new office, where I had partnered with a few guys and opened a subscription-based stock trading company. After all, this was right before the dot.com crash, and who wasn't making money trading stocks?

Once I moved out, the situation took a significant downturn. She did not want me back in the house and cut off most communication. I was devastated. In my mind, divorce was not an option. No one in my family had been divorced, and I was determined to fix this situation. This would be the first time in my life that, despite any level of effort or determination, I could not fix the situation. She was done, and I simply could not accept the prospect of raising children as separated parents. Being an exceptional father was by far the most important thing in my life.

Yet the war began, and the custody battle for the kids became the launching pad for the complete destruction of the relationship. I went into 100% victim mode, feeling sorry for myself. My behavior was like that of a little kid who had his candy taken away. I was operating completely on emotion.

During this period, neither of us produced any income. The dot. com crash was upon us. Between legal fees, investment losses and other expenses, we were burning our net worth at a rapid pace.

I was physically ill from the experience. I could not eat or sleep. I lost 40 pounds in three months and had to take Ambien to sleep at night. The battle became a "he said, she said" situation for all of our friends and family. To my complete surprise, most of our friends and even some of my own family came down on her side. Many people just avoided the situation. I was in disbelief that people who knew me for years and were well aware of my integrity and ethics, especially as a father, simply vanished.

I became distraught and hopeless and could not see a way out of the situation. I did not want to go outside for fear that I might have to confront someone. My heart was completely broken for my kids. I cried every day for months. My only allies were my parents; their nightly calls became my only support.

As it became more difficult for me to see my kids, I became desperate. Desperation means zero ability to apply any logic to the situation or engage in any reasonable thinking. I slipped into a deep state of darkness and concluded it was over. I was not going to survive this trauma. One evening in my warped sense of despair, when I went to take my Ambien to go to sleep, I dumped the bottle out and was prepared to take the coward's route to resolve the situation. I remember thinking that my kids would be better off without me. At that very moment, the phone rang, and it was my mother calling. That call got me out of the moment of desperation and kept me from doing the unimaginable.

In the coming months, I began to face reality, and my desperation faded. I began dating, and this helped restore my confidence. I built a few short-term, quality relationships that strengthened me.

However, I was still in a victim mindset when my father advised me to settle everything out of court, no matter what, to end the battle for the benefit of the kids. As hard as it was, I was only seeing my kids on the weekends. By this time, we had burned through most of life's savings and investments, but I agreed to everything she demanded to put an end to the madness. I made commitments in the settlement that I knew I could not keep. After all, I wasn't working, didn't have a business, and had zero income. Over the next few months, I paid for my child support and my kids' expenses from the little savings I had left from the settlement. The resolution I hoped for was slow to come about; seeing my way out of this quagmire was still almost impossible.

From victim to victor: The day my life changed forever!

"You gonna do something, or just stand there and bleed?"
--Tombstone, 1993

Just when the caterpillar thought the world was over, it became a beautiful butterfly!

September 11, 2001, I woke like any other day of the past year: depressed, feeling sorry for myself, with little hope. I lay in bed watching CNBC, as was my normal morning routine.

The legendary Mark Hanes was still the morning host when, at 8:46 am, the first plane hit the World Trade Center. At 9:02, the second plane hit the second tower. Like everyone else, sheer horror ripped through my heart. I knew thousands of people were in those buildings. Then, at 9:37, a plane hit the Pentagon.

Being in a suburb of Washington, a sense of panic set in. My first thought was my children, who should have all been in school at that time. I jumped in the car to get them, as did every other parent. Yet halfway to the school, I realized that if I picked them up, it would be a violation of my custody agreement. I would have more legal problems. I figured that my ex-wife was going to pick them up. I turned around and went home. Later in the day, as we realized the full extent of the terrorist attack, I actually went a second time to get my children, only to turn around once more at the thought of legal retribution.

I found out later that all four of my kids were among a mere handful of kids who were left at the school with no parent arriving to take them safely home.

I do not know what transpired inside of me, but imagining the pain my kids felt from that experience was the straw that broke the camel's back, as the saying goes. I spent that evening totally broken. Again, I felt helpless and completely inadequate as a parent for my kids. I had lost everything, including myself.

The combination of the effects of 9/11 and the culmination of the last 18 months of hell just came pouring out of me. I wept uncontrollably for hours. This was rock bottom! By 3:00 am, I nodded off.

The combined tragedy of 9/11 and my own rock-bottom combined in a powerful wake-up call. Overnight, for the first time in my life, I went from a child to a man. *I realized I was not alone; I had myself.*

When I opened my eyes the next day, I knew I could no longer be a victim to my ex-wife or to myself. I immediately started writing down my set of actions, and aggressive actions they were! The first of which was to completely end the relationship with my ex-wife permanently. I blocked my phone and email.

This was best for my kids, so they did not have to see the daily conflict. I knew I was an awesome dad, and starting at that moment, that was exactly what I was going to be.

I realized that I had always been good at making money and immediately started to strategize on how to build my next business.

Most importantly, I recognized that the woman I was dating was sent to me from heaven.

Up until this point, I leaned on other people to fill the gaps of my insecurities and relied on outside sources. This time, it was different. I was alone, with no friends, no support, and little hope. All I had was myself and that little bit of fire left in my soul that appeared overnight. This is where I made the transition from a reliant life to a reliable life, whereby I chose accountability for everything and began to rely on one person, *myself.* My outlook would never be a victim's again. Step by step, I took charge of everything, including myself. With each success, my confidence grew, and so did my self-esteem. I was a victor!

You must be a willing participant in your own resurrection.

I went on to marry the woman who was put on this Earth for me. We are 100% aligned in all of our values, goals, dreams, and desires. We don't compete on anything, and we complete everything…together. She is an amazing Mom to my four kids and the child we have together. We rebuilt an empire and replenished our finances in short order to millionaire status again. I built another business from scratch and after 19 years sold it for an 8-figure exit. The four kids from the marriage all went on to be amazing, productive adults, and all now have families of their own. I attribute this to both me and my ex-wife making parenting a priority in spite of the division between us.

As I stated earlier, no one is coming to the rescue but yourself. **Success is the best revenge.** Now that I can take full accountability for everything, I wish my ex-wife all the best. I find myself with no animosity, and the pain is a distant memory. I actually owe her a thank you for leading me to the path of an exceptional life. Who would ever imagine that this broke, insecure, victimized child-like man would build a life of love, relationships, and gratitude that most people wish for? I now approach everything as a two-way street: what's in it for us? I always want to bring as much value to a relationship as possible, especially my marriage.

"No one can go back and start a new beginning,
but anyone can start today and make a new ending."
--Maria Robinson

CHAPTER FOURTEEN

EMBRACE THE BATTLE

No quote from a fictional movie is more true than Rocky saying this to his son:

"Let me tell you something you already know. The world ain't all sunshine and rainbows. It's a very mean and nasty place, and I don't care how tough you are, it will beat you to your knees and keep you there permanently if you let it. You, me, or nobody is gonna hit as hard as life. But it ain't about how hard ya hit. It's about how hard you can get hit and keep moving forward. How much you can take and keep moving forward. That's how winning is done!"
- Sylvester Stallone, *Rocky Balboa*

If you are going into battle against anything, you must be prepared. You must have some idea what you are up against, both physically and mentally. No matter how much you prepare, study, and practice, be prepared for an effort required beyond anything you can imagine. You don't have to love the hard work; you just have to crave the result. I have some alarming news about your opponent, too. In the game of life, you will be facing your fiercest foe: *yourself.* I'm talking about the part of you that prefers comfort, certainty, quiet, and ease. The part that likes instant gratification. The part that would rather nap the day away because everything seems "good enough." The part that quits as soon as reality sets in. That inner Sheep may always stay with you, but learning the long-term rewards of being a Cheetah or even a Falcon will be a powerful motivator to keep that Sheepish voice quiet.

As I said, too many people don't *live*; they simply *exist*. Most of what you think of yourself is simply a lie you have fabricated to remain in a comfortable state. And you certainly can remain there. Most people do. But if you want more out of life, this is where the rubber meets the road. You must stray away from the familiar and charge forward to the place you envision for yourself. This means taking head on fear, risk, balance, being selfish, and, of course, suffering and pain. Here it is again: this means getting uncomfortable!

In order to make changes, you need to stop believing everything you think. Question everything.

Average is a sin; comfort is a curse!

> *"Change happens when the pain of staying the same*
> *is greater than the pain of change."*
> *--Tony Robbins*

Before we jump into the battle let's look as to why virtually everyone finds this process so difficult, if not impossible. Now, this is not to discourage you but for you to remember that you must always face the truth...and sometimes, the truth is hard to hear. Here's a hint: If hearing the truth makes you angry, then you know you are on your way to change.

Some of the most valuable lessons I have I had in my life came from someone who held their ground and spoke directly to me. I'll never forget when I was in the middle of my difficult divorce and a bitter custody battle, my therapist said to me, "Jerry, you need to grow up."

I was 40 years old at the time, and under those circumstances, hearing that advice totally pissed me off. However, it was years later that I realized he was completely spot-on with the truth. My victimized behavior at the time was completely childish. Today, I am thankful that he moved me in the right direction in my life.

As you embrace your battle to make your climb, there will be the need to change your habits. Changing habits and who and what you are made of is explained very well in two books, mentioned earlier, that I believe are must-reads for gaining a strategic advantage in your battle:

Atomic Habits by James Clear

Change Your Habits, Change Your Life by Tom Corley.

Both books give excellent guidance on the process of changing your mind and clearly explain the difficulty in doing so. Remember, get prepared for battle, and the more knowledge you have about the battlefield, the better advantage you can create, increasing your odds of a positive outcome.

Another bit of knowledge you will need to know is explained in the book *The Brain* by David Eagleman. I'm just going to touch on one concept from your childhood about your brain development, explaining why you think the way you think and the reasons behind who and what you are. This is the marble statue concept. Imagine that when you are born, your brain is a square slab of marble. Based on your experiences from birth to about 6 years old, the brain carves away about 50% of your brain connections called synapses. This process is called pruning of the brain; imagine chiseling the shape of your statue. We only keep the useful synapses based on our environment and experiences. You are then left with the marble statue that defines your being.

We don't grow into who we become. Rather, we evolve by what our brains eliminate or remove. The reason I bring this to your attention is to explain why it is so hard to change your thoughts and habits as adults. In order to do so, you need to add some marble that was chipped away back to your statue! No easy task.

You have probably figured out by now that if you want to live an exceptional life that is beyond the herd of the Sheep, there is a price to be paid. However, after many battles of my own, I do not consider it "price paid." Rather, I consider it enjoying the benefits of my efforts. Zig Ziglar, said "You don't pay the price for success; you enjoy the benefits." It's all about perception.

When you journey down this road and begin your battle, the entire process feels overwhelming and unattainable. As you slowly make the climb and start to accumulate small wins, the process will accelerate. What once was a dark tunnel that you blindly navigated, hitting obstacles along the way that you could not see, eventually opens to cracks of light that let you start to navigate a path to the next rung of the ladder. As counterintuitive as it may seem, the more willing you are to embrace the battle in front of you, the more likely you will eventually learn to love the battle. In here lies the secret to the climb. Learn to love the battle because you will learn to love the results.

As discussed, it's in our natural human nature to follow the path of least resistance. The climb to the top is to follow the path that yields results regardless of the obstacles that lie in that path. When choosing your path each day, you need to focus on short-term execution while maintaining your vision on what's way down the path, not what lies in the next few steps. Are you the type of person who would climb a new ladder every day of 20 rungs for $100 a day, or would you start your journey on a ladder of 10,000 rungs that may take years to climb but has a million dollars at the top? Almost everyone chooses a daily ladder of instant gratification versus the climb of accumulation. The Sheep need to know the check is coming on Friday. The 1% Cheetahs, Falcons, and Lions choose option two. It's called sacrifice!

In order to conquer those rungs upward on a steady basis and battle daily for your micro-wins, you will need to do what David Goggins refers to as "callousing your mind." Just like the hands of an Olympic power lifter or the balls of the feet of an ultra-marathon runner, a persistent pursuit of daily hard-fought wins will begin to train your mind to endure the challenges in front of you. Your mind is far more capable than you think.

In fact, most of us are only using about 40% of our brain's capacity while we'd swear we were at our utmost limits. You may have become comfortable with low levels of performance and have therefore trained yourself to be soft. If you want to win these daily battles with yourself, you will need to learn how to be hard on yourself.

"Success takes a backbone, not a wishbone."
--Brad Lee

One technique I use is to make agreements or contracts with myself. As part of my commitment to ethics, I am unwilling to break a contract or commitment with anyone - so why would I break it with myself? Build in a little reward or break for keeping your contract with yourself. This will help you get started. Do this a few times, and you will no longer need to reward yourself because the reward will be built into the benefits of the results. Once this process starts to happen, you will be on your way to callousing your mind. Your mind will become more durable, dependable, and programmed to execute. Furthermore, this callousing process of your mind will lead you to having your logical mind dominate your feelings and emotions.

Pain and I have become best friends

"Pain will leave you once it's done teaching you."
--Bruce Lee

Throughout this book I have discussed the necessary need to develop your ability to endure pain and suffering. Eventually, whether self-inflicted or from outside sources, you will be thrown into this arena multiple times in your life. Believe me, preparing in advance how to endure the pain and suffering that is coming your way is a true characteristic of high achievers. As you callous your mind, as discussed in David Goggins "Can't Hurt Me," you will be able to not only endure the pain and suffering of random events in your life, but you will be better for it. Eventually, your mind will anticipate difficult situations and start reacting in some sense of normalcy instead of panic and desperation.

We have all heard of "the zone" as it relates to sports, but the zone goes beyond sports; it translates into your mental capacity to be engaged in any difficult situation, whereby your logical mind puts you in control no matter how challenging the task before you. Just ask a Navy Seal the importance of maintaining a disciplined mind that produces clarity and functions to perfection under the most adversarial conditions. You will learn to train yourself to know that eventually, "it will be alright," and therefore, your levels of fear and anxiety are under control. I think we can all agree that this would be a wonderful place to be.

The fights to win these battles are a war between you and you. No one is coming to the rescue, so I want you to immediately stop looking for an outside source to fight the battle for you or with you. This battle is an inside job, and the pressure to succeed is a privilege. You earned the opportunity; it was not given to you. You, and only you, must do the work – only you *can* do the work! Instead of looking for others to support you and help you up your ladder, take this approach. Who can I bring up the ladder with me? When you engage in complete accountability and responsibility, others will look up to you for leadership and guidance.

I like to call it being the "go-to" person in your job, business, family, and community. I'm from a large family, and when growing up, I saw all the time that when we had issues/crises or when family members needed any type of advice in our family, my dad was the go-to guy who everyone could count on to execute and do the right thing. This gave me a sense of security and an understanding of leadership when growing up. In his book *The Power of One More*, Ed Mylett calls this being "The One." The one in your family that makes generational change by winning these battles for financial independence and leadership.

> *"A leader is one who knows the way,*
> *goes the way, and shows the way."*
> -John C. Maxwell

Pain and sacrifice become distant memories and will dissipate in your past. The beneficial results of pain and sacrifice will endure in your future forever. Nothing worthwhile in life is achieved without desire, commitment, execution, and an uncompromising determination to succeed. It's the way the human spirit was constructed from the beginning of time. Accept it unknowingly as a powerful force of human nature, for it will never change and is ingrained deep within our souls.

Bodybuilding: the 30-year project

> *"Wins and losses come a dime a dozen. But effort? Nobody can judge that. Because effort is between you and you."*– Ray Lewis

I thought I was "all in" in many ways in my life, but I was about to find out what "all in" really meant!

As my golf career wound down, I started spending more time in the gym. Down the street from the University of Maryland, and near my apartment, was a gym called Dynamo. It was, to say the least, a meathead gym – a place where you might see Rocky training. The equipment was old, some of it was even rusty, and the gym was 90% free weights. There was no staff, and you could enter using combination lock on the door 24 hours a day.

As you can imagine, the members were mostly power-lifters and wannabe bodybuilders. There I was, at 5' 10" and a thin 155 pounds. I certainly did not fit the mold physically, but I learned in short order that I fit in mentally. I was willing to do the work!

I immediately put my Observer skills to use, seeking knowledge from some of the seasoned weight lifters who were regulars. Although, it was embarrassing to ask these well-trained men for help with my bench press of a mere 150 pounds. Well, I was determined to do something about that as soon as possible.

I set a goal of bench pressing 185 pounds. In free weight terms, this means two 45-pound plates and two 25-pound plates on the bar, which itself weighed 45 pounds. I got a few workout routines to increase strength from a few of the guys I had met there. I also learned from them about the value of protein and weight gainer supplements. In a few short months, I reached my goal, and then set my sights on bench pressing 225 pounds, which meant four 45-pound plates on the bar, two on each side. I got my body weight up to 170 pounds, and over the next six months, I hit that bench-pressing goal as well.

I started to notice other benefits to my efforts. I felt great physically and mentally. My confidence soared as I saw the physical benefits of how I looked, and others noticed, too. My dating life was vastly improved.

I should point out that my drive, determination, and motivation all accelerated from my short-term success. Again, action preceded motivation. I overcame my reputation of being a "short hitter" in my golf game. Thanks to my increased lower-body strength, I added more than 30 yards to my drive. This made me consider making another run at my golf career. But due to many other non-compatible goals happening in my life at the time, it was not meant to be.

The gold standard in the gym was set by the guys who could bench 300 pounds or more. Weighing only 170 myself, and being far from being a genetically gifted weightlifter, I set a goal to one day bench 300 pounds. It was somewhat laughable and seemed impossible at the time, so I kept this goal to myself. I kept watching, learning, and working hard for years, but I was stuck in the 280-pound range.

And there I stayed until I met the owner of a new gym I was going to. I told him my goals, and we started working together. After ten years of failures and setbacks, I finally nailed my 300-pound bench press at the age of 35.

This was a great moment, but in its aftermath, I made a significant mistake.

I'll never forget the feeling of euphoria, the day I cleanly bench pressed 300 lbs. This was in the works for a decade. Yet after leaving the gym that day, I distinctly remember that euphoria transition into a nagging, "Okay, but what now?"

I felt like my weightlifting days were over, my goal achieved. Outside of plans for my business, I had nothing else lined up as a major goal or target in my life at that time.

Without that target in mind, I slipped into bad habits. I began eating fast food and drinking more, and as you can guess, I was rarely at the gym. I gained weight – but for the wrong reasons – until I weighed 190 pounds.

Life has phases and stages. When one phase ends, you must have another horizon to aim for, or you will slip into the abyss. This is why healthy and permanent weight loss is so difficult for many people: they set a goal, like, "I want to lose 40 pounds before my class reunion." Or before their wedding or their vacation. Fill in the blank. They have a specific date in mind, a specific reason for changing their habits. And indeed, they may lose the weight, but once the event comes and goes, they no longer have that goal in mind. Old, bad habits return, and the weight comes back. This is a common example, but by no means the only way in which people let themselves lapse into comfortable (yet harmful) habits. Mentally, if we don't have something to aim for, we tend to simply take the path of least resistance. The climb up the ladder required being uncomfortable for a lifetime. Although this sounds detrimental to living any reasonable quality life, you will learn to be comfortable being uncomfortable!

In my case, those negative lifestyle changes lasted about five years until my divorce when I was 40. I hit rock bottom.

Only after meeting the woman who would later become my wife and change my life forever for the positive did I get back to what had worked. My new wife was an avid gym-goer, and we were off to the races. In short order, I set a goal to bench press 315 pounds.

As this means three 45-pound plates on each side of the bar, this is often referred to as "triple donuts." It's another gold-standard number, aspired to by most weightlifters with body weights under 200 pounds. Remember, I'd increased my body weight to 190 pounds…for the wrong reasons. Although the extra weight helped me move more weight and endure the hard workouts, I was faced with the exact same problems I'd had when striving to bench press 300 pounds. I was stuck in the low 300s for years, regardless of my relentless efforts. I walked away from that goal multiple times, only to come back to it, more determined.

When I turned 50, I rejoined a small gym that was known for powerlifting and bodybuilding. I discussed my goal with one of the trainers who worked with powerlifters. He gave me a workout routine specifically designed to increase the strength in the muscles to increase my bench press.

This was a heavy workout: five days a week, varying the exercises. He structured it as a three-month program. And yes, magically, in three months, I did it! I bench-pressed 315 pounds!

Just kidding. There was no magic involved – unless dedication, determination, sweat, and seeking the advice of an expert can be considered magic.

After years of hard work, commitment, nutrition, and supplemental education, I eventually bench-pressed 350 pounds with my own body weight remaining at 190 pounds. Statistically, I don't consider that remarkable – but personally, it was quite an achievement. I was certainly not gifted genetically to ever be able to reach that pinnacle. Extremely hard work and dedication got me there.

Do you see commonality in these long-term achievements? This entire process was a 30-year project that involved setbacks, pivots, and resilience. I had elbow and shoulder surgery, each of which pushed me back six months. I even walked away from these goals for years a couple of times only to be reenergized for the comeback, and the comeback is always greater than the setback.

Discipline is the strongest form of self-love.

Both of these long-term achievements required an expert in their field to push my results past the finish line. Seeking coaching and experience is essential to all execution and growth. Both people who pushed me to the end result were coaches who had been in the trenches and performed at high levels. They were seasoned professionals. Surround yourself with them!

Remember, however, that after meeting one horizon, you should always have another horizon lined up behind it. Well, I had no idea what was in store for me next.

Battle of my lifetime

When I was in my early fifties, I noticed a new trainer at my small gym. You couldn't miss this guy. He was huge. Six-foot-two, 270 pounds, and a little intimidating, with lots of muscle mass and these interesting artistic tattoos. This was no average trainer, he worked with an elite class of experienced weightlifters, and many of them were women. The workouts they were doing made mine look like a walk in the park.

After a few more weeks of observation, I figured out that he was training bodybuilders and bikini competitors. Of course, I was intrigued. Not only by the guys who were cut like statues, but the girls were even more impressive; they looked like fitness models in magazines.

I had been working out for over thirty years at this point, but I didn't look anything like his clients. This was a serious dude. He was almost abusive toward clients who weren't performing to his standards. He didn't care who was in the gym or what anyone else thought. He would get in his client's faces and make them suffer or, "You need to fucking quit!" His words.

It wasn't uncommon to hear him yelling in front of the whole gym. The guy was results-driven and you had better be on board with that. Without ever speaking a word to him, I knew he was authentic, and that he was aligned with my results-driven beliefs.

During the first month, he never gave me any notice, even though I was there every day. No, "Hey, how are you doing?" Or even a nod in my direction.

I always worked out early on Sunday mornings. On this particular Sunday, he was there with ten clients doing a bodybuilding posing clinic. The women were to die for, and the guys who had shows coming up were ripped and shredded like I'd never seen in person before.

My wife always liked using personal trainers. We couldn't work out together due to our schedules, so she was in the market for a trainer.

Good personal trainers are hard to find (remember my 10% rule), but I knew this guy was the real deal, so I decided to make this happen. Janna was a hard worker. She enjoyed being pushed to the limits.

So, I explained to Janna how hardcore this guy was, and she said, "Bring it on."

As intimidating as it was, I approached Major Payne and asked if he had any openings. But much to my relief, he was as polite as can be. First impressions can be deceiving. David was actually quite a friendly guy who was super intense about his profession. Special people have special problems, and David was no different.

A week later, he began training with my wife. He always treated Janna with respect because she would always do the required work without complaining. David hated complainers. I even saw him kick some clients right out of the gym. After a few months, I decided that I should give it a go, too. I knew this would be difficult, but I had spent my whole life seeking "hard." A challenge like this was right up my alley.

Thus began my journey into the bodybuilding world.

David was a heavyweight, competitive bodybuilder who won multiple bodybuilding championships. His clients dominated the local circuit. He even had some bodybuilders make it to the professional ranks. David was a total pro who had been deep in the trenches. This is who you seek advice from!

I found out he had a degree in philosophy and was very well-educated in human biology. He knew exactly how to prescribe diet and nutrition for growth and leanness. He was a fact-based logic guy with little emotion in the equation.

A Falcon or Lion is excellent with details. That's the level David had reached in the bodybuilding world.

We'd been working with him for about six months. I felt great and was getting results.

Then I told him something I'd been thinking about for some time. "David, I've been busting my ass in the gym for over thirty years and look nothing like these bodybuilder guys you train."

He simply said, "Oh, you want to go down that path?"

He asked me to take my shirt off and did a quick analysis of me.

He said, "You have plenty of muscle mass; you just can't see it. It's lying under all the fat you have. You've been eating wrong for thirty years. Once you develop the muscle mass, it's all about the diet."

The gym walls were filled with pictures of all of the competitors who actually made it to the stage.

David said, "Do you want your picture up there?"

"Sure," I said ignorantly. "How do I get started?"

He laughed, "Do you realize that this will be the hardest thing you've ever done in your life? Only ten percent of people who attempt this actually make it to the stage."

That's all I needed to hear. Tell me how hard it is and that I can't do it, and I'll show you what I'm made of.

He put me on an eight-week sample diet, similar to what a bodybuilding prep diet might look like.

David said, "For the next eight weeks, you will eat this exact diet in these exact portions. Not one bite of anything else goes in your body. No cheating, and absolutely no alcohol. You will be hungry!"

The diet was super bland and highly repetitive. It only included four things as main portions: chicken, fish, egg whites, Greek yogurt, and small amounts of carbs from rice, potatoes, and vegetables. Fish, egg whites, and yogurt were foods I never ate and never liked. I immediately asked him if I could substitute them for something else.

He laughed again, "I told you. Only ten percent. You should quit now!"

I made the commitment, but only three or four days into the prep diet I began to suffer. My body and brain had been programmed for decades. Those cravings and habits do not change overnight. I soon realized that this was going to be grueling, but I had made the commitment, so I was ready for battle.

After about the fourth week, I started to notice some changes. My energy was up, I was waking up earlier, I had a better attitude, and I felt a little more energized in the gym.

I'm not going to lie. It was really fucking hard. The most challenging thing was the change in lifestyle. For eight weeks, I never ate out at a restaurant and never stopped at a convenience store. I had to pack my food and have it with me at all times. This is really hard on your social life because the easiest way to avoid temptation is to stay away from it. The few times I did have to be somewhere with friends or family, yes, I took my food with me.

When I completed eight weeks, I started to notice a bit more muscle definition. I had dropped eight pounds of body weight, about one pound a week.

The Consultation

David sat down with me and explained that the eight-week sample diet was my test.

He said, "You completed it with one hundred percent discipline, so you say, with not a single bite of anything off-plan, so you have a small chance of making it. As hard as that was, the actual prep process runs for four months. That'll be even more taxing. It will require a mental discipline that only a certain few individuals possess. At the same time, we're doing a six-day-a-week weight training workout. You will also do a five-day-a-week cardio workout during a controlled starvation process. As hard as you think this will be, multiply it by a hundred. It's nothing short of self-inflicted torture. Are you sure you want to do this, Jerry?"

The more he tried to talk me out of it, the more I was all in. This conversation took place in June. The game plan was to hit the Maryland

State Bodybuilding Championships stage the following spring in late April.

The game plan was to increase muscle mass from June through December with a specific mass-building diet and workout, then start the show prep on January first. This also gave me time to factor the prep into my personal schedule. I planned no trips, no weekend getaways, and no business commitments for the fifteen weeks of prep. The summer and fall went well, and I gained some size, especially in my lower body which was my weaker area. I added about six pounds of increased muscle mass when the January date arrived.

The 50-Year Lie

> *"Today, I will do what others won't,*
> *so tomorrow, I can do what others can't."*
> – Jerry Rice

Although the program was laid out clear as day, for some reason, I just ignored the cardio aspect of the prep. Subconsciously, I just didn't think it was that important. The lesson here is that no matter how well you are prepared mentally for any challenge, the reality can be quite different. Remember, you don't know what you don't know.

David gave the starting cardio program for the first month, which consisted of five days a week, 30 minutes per day, at 60 steps per minute on the step mill. The step mill was the go-to cardio equipment for the bodybuilding world, due to no impact and a high calorie burn rate. It's an electronically propelled rotating set of stairs which can be set by steps per minute.

I had never been on one in my life, and there was another problem. I was not a cardio guy. I had never even run a mile in my life. When playing sports as a kid, I was the last place guy who walked at the end of the workouts. I always believed I had poor lungs and breathing capacity. I told David my cardio limitations, and he just laughed again and said, "Quit now!"

I was about to learn one of the greatest lessons of my life from my belief that I was unable to do cardio. David changed my plan to start at just 5 minutes a day every day on the step mill at a slow pace of 30 steps per minute. He told me that no matter what happened, I had to finish the 5 minutes, even if I had to lower the pace. He was firm at that point and told me, "Throughout this process, you will finish everything. You cannot quit or fail to finish, not even once!"

Five minutes was absolute torture for me, but I kept going according to plan. The next week, it was 10 minutes per day with increased intensity. This process went on for the first six weeks. Suddenly one day, I was up to 20 minutes at 60 steps per minute, and when the 20 minutes was up, I felt like I could do more, so I stayed on an extra five minutes. The rest of the story is history.

As my conditioning improved and my weight dropped from the diet plan, I found myself able to do an hour on the step mill at a pace of 80 steps per minute. I also worked in an intense interval called hit-cardio, where I ran on the step mill for a minute and backed off for a minute. Throughout this entire prep, I finished my planned workouts no matter what.

The invaluable lesson I learned was that I had made up a lie about myself that persisted for 50 years! Although not a genetically gifted cardio athlete, I simply did not push long and hard enough to get the required results. The reason this was so enlightening is that I then asked myself, *what else have I been lying to myself about for 50 years?* This was a life-changing question.

The Diet

"A lot of us don't know about another world that exists for us because it's on the other side of suffering. That's the real growth in life."
--David Goggins

When David told me that this endeavor would be the hardest thing I've ever done, my reply was, "I've done a lot of hard shit. How hard can it be?"

He just smiled and said, "We will see what you're made of."

Just like every other challenging comment he made, this just made me more determined to show him I was a warrior. Little did I know that the path I was about to take would push my limits beyond anything I had ever experienced.

What I did not understand was that this was not a goal I controlled. Rather, it controlled me, and I had to determine how to respond to it. The difference between this and anything I had ever done before is that there would be no break, no reprieve, and no relief from the pain and suffering for 15 weeks, 24 hours a day, 7 days a week.

The bodybuilding prep diet is a biological scientific approach on the way to reducing body fat and maintaining muscle mass to create the optimal body for the stage. It takes a seasoned expert who has been in the trenches for years to design, implement, and manage the process. David looked at his clients like a piece of art that he was creating. Each human body reacts differently, and David was a pro at adapting to the results. He based it on a detailed analysis of weekly check-in numbers and weekly photos to monitor the progress, adjusting as necessary.

I had full confidence that I was working with the best.

When you know you have the right coach, listen, shut up, and do what you're told. Knowing you have hired the right person makes it imperative that you put your faith in them. You can discuss the why's for your own self-satisfaction and education, but do not question the methods of a proven Alpha Lion.

The pain when your mind and body are starved for carbs and fats is pure torture. There is no escape. The battle rages 24 hours a day with little relief. There is no way for me to describe the pain and mental torture of doing heavy workouts on virtually no carbs. I became very irritable, and I quickly realized it was best for me to be *alone*. When you take the last bite of one of your six meals a day, you immediately start looking forward to the next meal, wondering how you are going to make it. Life became an hourly battle of survival, pushing my mental discipline to places I had never been before.

I'll never forget that at 12 weeks into the prep, I was getting ready for my weekly check-in pictures. When I looked in the mirror, I said, "Holy shit, is that me?" I was suffering so badly and felt so depleted from the diet and hard workouts that I considered quitting multiple times. I couldn't sleep because when your body fat goes below 10% you can't hold water, and you need to urinate about every hour. I remember calling David one night and asking him, "Are you sure I'm not going to die?"

However, I looked amazing, so I capitalized on that motivation. This was another epiphany moment that gave me an idea. I had a collection of classic and exotic cars, with my favorite being my Lamborghini Huracan. Since my body didn't seem like it belonged to me, I decided it didn't. I imagined that my body was the Lamborghini, and my mind was responsible for taking care of not only how it looked but how it was fueled and performed. Your mind is a powerful thing that can be convinced of just about everything. From that point forward I looked at my body separately from my mind and made sure my body was taken care of just like it was a Lamborghini.

About a month out from the show, I started focusing on the end in sight. This thought of only four more weeks made the pain and suffering more tolerable. David was pleased with my progress and my overall look. In fact, he said I was developing better than he'd anticipated. Any bit of encouragement coming from David was rare, and his little comment about my progress was just what the doctor ordered at the perfect moment.

Victory: Living for the moment
Make no mistake about it; life is a battle.
Instead of trying to avoid the battle, embrace it!
Once you learn to love the battle, you will learn to love the results.

I competed in the Classic division. Men's bodybuilding has three divisions: physique, classic and full bodybuilding. I was not genetically thick and big enough to move right into the bodybuilding division, and my legs were definitely not up to those standards, but I had enough size to compete in the middle classic division.

In classic competition, one's symmetry and definition (how shredded you are) are scored higher than overall size. David explained that judging at these events varied quite a bit. Not only the judges but who else showed up in my division were factors in how I would place.

"Bring your best and let the chips fall where they will," he said. He emphasized controlling what was in my control. Since he felt I would be outsized on the stage, I would need to be a better conditioned athlete if I expected a top-five finish.

I understood exactly what he was talking about. Who was willing to put in the extra work related to cardio and diet to be the leanest, most shredded competitor? And then he said, "Jerry, it's the only strategic advantage you can get."

Again, I listened carefully. Fully trusting David, I increased my cardio to two sessions per day. David trimmed my diet to create the perfect balance of lean muscle mass to match my 6% body fat. Two weeks out, I was in the home stretch, and even though the pain and suffering were brutal, I could see the end in sight. I also had confidence that I could get a top-five finish. However, this belief was from a place of ignorance since I had no experience on the stage. But I looked good, and the other experienced bodybuilders in the gym were impressed as well.

Another epiphany; At about 10 days out, I was on the step mill doing the first of the two hour-long cardio sessions for my day. It hit me like a ton of bricks. This thought dated back 35 years: in my golf career, I never won a tournament after the age of 18 when Junior golf ended. I had several 2nd place and top ten finishes, but the bitterness of the wins that escaped me suddenly became front and center in my mind. What if I finished second? Just the thought of a second-place finish shattered my soul to the core. Oh no, not again! For the last 10 days, my all-encompassing focus was what David told me: I must out-condition the competition. The step mill and I became best friends.

The final week before a competition means fine-tuning the creation and perfecting your posing routine. The trick is to be as lean as possible but to look as full as possible related to your muscle mass. That is also a process that must be left to the experts. The week was set up with light workouts and moderate cardio. My diet included increasing my carbs three days out, which increases muscle volume and physical appearance by increasing glycogen storage. To get my skin's appearance as thin as possible to increase the visible amount of muscle definition, I depleted my water intake starting 36 hours before stage time.

Show day began at 5:00 am with a scheduled time for spray tanning. I had no idea what to expect, but when I arrived for my appointment in the basement of the arena, the halls were lined with spray tanning tents. Most of the people doing the tanning were women. You must be buck-naked to tan properly so there are no visible lines around your show attire. The entire process was bizarre! It took 30 minutes of me standing there absolutely naked in front of a young lady. Some of the women getting sprayed were walking around topless as if the guys were not even in the room.

I took it all in, then went back to my hotel room for my two ounces of peanut butter on a rice cake before heading to the backstage area around 9:00 am. My class wasn't scheduled until 1:00 pm, but all competitors were required to hang out backstage until their time slot. I did what I always do: observe and listen. I was definitely one of the oldest competitors in the competition and received several compliments from some of the more seasoned competitors on how I looked for my age. Although I was absolutely terrified to hit that stage, this did give me a little preshow confidence. I also overheard some of the classic competitors in the division I was competing in discussing their cardio prep routines. They were bragging about the 45-minute, 5-day-a-week cardio they did. I did double that, and this knowledge also lifted my confidence.

When we got the call for Classic B to line up for the walk to the stage, I got my first glimpse of my competition. My 5'9.5" height put me in this class. I felt I was definitely the best-conditioned athlete but not the largest in muscle mass.

And out we went.

As bodybuilders move through their posing routines, the judges move them around. The person who finishes in the center of the group is usually the winner. I started in the middle and was never moved! However, being in the middle does not guarantee you are the winner because, in the evening routine, the judges can adjust. At the night show, contestants do a posing routine to music, and of course, I chose "Inside I Stand Alone" by Godsmack. After the routines, they announced the winners. I was crowned the Maryland State Bodybuilding Champion in my class.

The feeling of euphoria was like nothing I had ever experienced. I realized that my ability to endure the suffering and pain for so long had a direct correlation to the emotional euphoric result. The more difficult the task, the greater the reward. And such is life!

Initially, my goal was simply to get on the stage, but as the process moved along, the action and dedication elevated my motivation. I adapted and changed my vision. This win buried a lot of old demons for me that would never return again. This experience propelled my life in ways that I never imagined. I've never looked at any challenge put before me as impossible again.

In fact, the ability to battle though the misery of this process left me feeling like I could do anything. Things I previously saw as difficult became relative to the comparison of the prep process, and I doubt I will ever be faced with anything that difficult again. Now, everything seems possible and achievable. Just like making the golf team 35 years earlier, this was another million-to-one shot that came true because I chose to be in the game.

Over the next three years, I went on to take four first-place finishes in various classes in the bodybuilding world. None of this glory would have been possible without the high-level coaching from David Johnston. Associate with winners for the win!

> *"I could have missed the pain,*
> *but I would have had to miss the dance."*
> – Garth Brooks

I am often asked why I – why *anyone* – would voluntarily subject themselves to such pain and suffering. And my answer is simple: **Our struggles determine our strengths and our strengths lift us to glory!**

By voluntarily subjecting yourself to extremely difficult challenges, which push you to your limits and beyond, you will be prepared for when the time comes when it's not voluntary. Whether you choose your difficulty or if its thrust upon you, one thing I can guarantee you in your life is that call, that crisis, that setback is coming your way.

Choose to become unbreakable!

"True self-esteem has to be earned with scar tissue."

--Dan Pena

CHAPTER FIFTEEN

INSIDE, I STAND ALONE

*You can't love yourself if you don't know yourself, and you
can't know yourself if you don't spend time with yourself.*
-Ed Mylett

Before we get into what this chapter is all about, let's quickly discuss what it's *not* about. The concept of "standing alone" has nothing to do with being a loner or limiting your relationships. No one climbs their ladder alone.

Virtually every great thing that has ever happened to me has stemmed from relationships, both good and bad. Every great success and tragic failure has a name listed next to it!

Over your lifetime, you will be able to look back, just as I have, and identify those key mentors, coaches, partners, and yes, even Snakes, who contributed to your success. Many of those associations will not have been good ones. There is just as much, if not more, to learn from your bad relationships and associations with Snakes than those relationships with Cheetahs, Falcons, and Lions. From our observations and interactions with all these types, we develop our inner moral core.

Who is responsible for you? Your parents? Your boss? Your spouse? The government? Your doctor? Your friends? I think by now you know what my response will be.

Life is a game of *you* versus *you*. You are 100% independently responsible for every outcome, regardless of all circumstances. Read *Can't Hurt Me* by David Goggins, then let's hear your counterargument.

There isn't one! Keep promises to yourself first, and build a reputation with yourself. Be careful what you say because you are listening.

Accountability in all things

"No one will ever know the violence it took to become this gentle."
--Ralph Waldo Emerson

I learned that I had reached the pinnacle of accountability in an unfortunate, unique experience. I am an avid car collector of both exotic and classic cars. As a standard practice, I used to go to my office on Sunday mornings from about 6:00-9:00am to catch up on the week. I loved this alone time.

If the weather was good, it was my habit to take one of the cars from my collection every Sunday. That particular week, I took my '69 Resto Mod ZL1 Camaro: an orange beauty with classic Crager wheels, ghost-style custom paint job, and powerful 502 cubic inch engine that cranked out about 600 horses. She was a former Barrett Jackson auction car.

When I left my office, I headed out to the main road, which was one lane each way with a double yellow line and a speed limit of 45. As I was driving down the road, an oncoming Acura right in front of me tried to make a U-turn. I had no chance to respond and T-boned the car in the center of the passenger door.

It's amazing what your mind can think of in less than two seconds! My first thought before the impact was, "Oh shit, the airbag!" but then I realized I was driving a 1969 model.

Then I thought, "Am I wearing my seat belt?" I was.

My mind then quickly transferred to this terrible realization: "If there is someone in the passenger seat of that, Acura, I am going to kill them." The Acura's windows were blackout-tinted and I had no idea if someone was in the passenger seat.

My final thought was, *relax to take the impact.* My instinct from my sports history served me well. I hit him so hard that it launched the Acura off the ground.

The Acura landed facing the opposite direction. Without hesitation, the driver took off, and I had a hit-and-run on my hands. A witness took off after him and got the tag number. (Yes, keep the faith; the world is full of good Samaritans.)

I was fortunate that I was not hurt except being bruised from my seat belt. My beautiful Camaro was potentially totaled.

Then something amazing took place. My mind immediately started thinking about what I could have done to avoid the situation. Why was I there at that specific time? If only I had antilock brakes! Why this car on this day? I wasn't angry at the other guy; I wasn't devastated about my car. I was calm and accepted full accountability for a random incident that was out of my control, knowing that life's random, unexpected events are simply part of the game. This is the day I knew I made it to the pinnacle of complete accountability.

Your inner moral core

> *"Strive not to be a success, but rather to be of value."*
> --Albert Einstein

Your inner moral core is essentially your personal value system. It belongs to only you. You are the sole captain of its journey. When it is fully developed, you have reached your pinnacle. You, and you alone, are accountable for every decision and its outcome, whether these things are in your control or outside of it.

The inner moral core is an integrated part of yourself. Developing an inner moral core to its full potential will make your climb up the ladder a more stable, consistent process. On the inside, it is your ethics, principles, and morals. On the outside, it is your character. Remember, in life, it does not matter what we say or even what we think. What we *do* is all that matters; your inner moral core is your guide to *doing* what aligns with your inviolate principles.

Where most people get off track is the violation of an inner principle because they suffer doubt or insecurity. They seek a quick fix, a short-term financial gain or exploited relationship that bolsters their ego. But these things are temporary and lead to greater doubt and insecurity than ever before.

Sticking with your core beliefs is easier said than done. Anyone can write down the principles that make up your inner moral core. In fact, that is a great start. But as you know, I am all about the truth, and acknowledgment of the principles you desire to follow is only the start.

The reality is that developing a *strong* inner moral core, one that does not sway under the pressure of doubt or insecurity, is a lengthy, arduous process. Your elders can attest to this: often, it takes years to internalize the values of who you are and what you are made of.

Just like evolving toward the characteristics of successful people, you must evolve toward following the principles that make your inner moral core by slowly, over time, changing how you internalize your strengths, and how doing so manifests in your external thoughts, decision-making and related actions.

Focus on, look for, and recognize a positive trend to see the slow changes over time in your ability to do what's right in the face of adversity or peer pressure. When everyone around you panics, follows the crowd, or makes the wrong choice (as Sheep often do), but you manage to remain steadfast in your beliefs, recognize your achievement. Take note of how good it feels to do the right thing. Remember what we learned about authenticity. No one will be able to sway you from that feeling of vindication.

As the process matures, you will trust yourself more. That trust will give you the willpower to hold your ground firmly.

Many times, these decisions will have negative short-term ramifications related to finances, relationships, and your self-esteem. However, let me make this perfectly clear: standing your ground for what you think is right, regardless of the short-term consequences, wins in the long run every time.

Accelerating up your ladder requires losses that may be painful at the moment. Sometimes, we need to wait a long time for this all to come to fruition, but I assure you if you stick with your core values and principles, it will!

As you gain experience over years of time, your inner moral core may also require some change. This is normal, as you cannot value experiences and situations that you have not faced yet. An inner moral core must be flexible enough to accept new wisdom. For example, I assure you that you will place a different value on your marriage after 30 years than when you are a newlywed. Disappointments, setbacks, manipulations, betrayals, crises, and how you address the related recoveries to these events in your life will all contribute to who you will be on the inside.

Happiness is an inside job.

Imagine a puppy: the inner moral core as man's best friend

"I do not wish any reward but to know I have done the right thing."
--Mark Twain

As you know by now, I use metaphors to keep myself in line. This concept is no exception! I like to think of my inner moral core as a living, separate entity that I will carry with me for eternity. I see it as a puppy: an honest, faithful, companion who is loyal to the end, but who needs my care and love to thrive.

I get some ribbing from my wife and others when I use the "puppy" analogy to describe something that needs our constant care and attention. But I can hardly think of a better example!

A mistake that many people make when it comes to their inner moral core is assuming that it is something that develops on its own, independently of our actions. They assume that a strong moral core is something a person either has or doesn't have, failing to remember that *everything* about us, be it physical, mental, or spiritual, must be cared for and cultivated if we want it to reach its full potential. Our inner moral core must be strengthened and honed to guide us even against the most powerful social pressure: following the crowd. Going along with the "norm," even when the norm is wrong, can be humankind's most dangerous failing. Few people have the strength to stand against the tide that sweeps the Sheep along. Train your puppy well!

"A lie doesn't become truth, wrong doesn't become right, and evil doesn't become good, just because it's accepted by a majority."
--Booker T. Washington

Think of the most morally upstanding people you know – do you suppose they never make a mistake? Never were tempted to take the easy way? Never had to deny their instant gratification in favor of a long-term reward? Of course, these things happened to them. But they *attend* to their inner moral core and give it as much attention as we would give any vulnerable creature in our care. Thus, when it comes time to do the right thing – even when they stand alone – they can recognize what it is and follow their best instincts.

So let's talk about the puppy, because visualizing my inner moral core in this way reminds me daily that I need to take care of it. Remember, you can convince your mind of just about anything with repeated belief through self-talk. I imagine that I have a little puppy inside me that needs to be loved, fed, cared for, taught, and led. I check how it is doing throughout the day and tuck it in nicely at night. The care that you give it will be returned tenfold as it guides and protects you.

When you get that uneasy feeling in your gut from making an unethical decision, it's a sign that your inner moral core is suffering. If you keep violating your moral core, your puppy will eventually get sick. How sick it feels and your related discomfort will be in direct proportion to your failed principles. A chronically sick inner moral core leads to a miserable life. When you meet a Snake, you can be assured they have failed to care for that creature within; it is now riddled with disease and parasites, and its prognosis for recovery is slim due its chronic poor habits and related health.

It's in our nature to want to help Snakes change who they are and give them a second chance. We want to heal and help the sick. Heed this warning: you cannot save everyone, and it's not your obligation to do so. Your personal inner moral core is your only obligation, and that obligation is to one's self.

Of course, this requires living from a position of good intentions, high personal standards, and building the architecture of your inner moral core daily. Gaining and recognizing short-term wins feeds your inner moral core. Engaging in regimented daily habits like going to the gym, self-learning, nurturing relationships, and daily achievements will all lend themselves to nurturing and slowly building your inner moral core until it becomes unbreakable.

The highest courage is to dare yourself in the face of adversity. Choosing right over wrong, ethics over convenience, and truth over popularity … these are the choices that will measure your life and

your legacy. Travel the path of integrity without looking back, for there is never a wrong time to do the right thing.

Are you comfortable being alone with yourself?

"Being alone has a power that very few people can handle."
--Steven Aitchison

Many of you may remember Aaron Rodgers, the famous Green Bay Packers quarterback, went on a "darkness retreat," to isolate himself and figure out his future. He was not seeking external advice, consultation, or guidance, he was seeking to learn within himself.

The process is called "sensory-deprivation isolation," whereby people spend a few days in total darkness, away from electronics, other people, and most external stimuli, and thus are utterly alone with their thoughts.

Being isolated completely by yourself is something that highly successful people do not fear. Whether it's a hiking trip, a vacation, or even just going to the movies alone, solitude should not be an uncomfortable place. Yet many of us are quite resistant, even terrified, of the idea of being alone. If the idea of being alone makes you anxious, take a harder look at your inner moral core. Are you taking care of it, nurturing it, and letting it guide you in return? Remember, when you are alone, you are not alone...you are with yourself. Do you like your companion?

What you think and what you do when you are alone will tell you a great deal about yourself. Maybe far more than you expected. An escape like this is an effective way to measure who you are inside and find out if you are good with yourself. It is imperative to be good with yourself and your private thought processes if you are going to be good for other people. When you gain high self-esteem and are secure within yourself, it will lead to the principle of attraction, whereby you will attract what you are seeking. You will also have the inner strength to avoid what you are not seeking, regardless of how attractive it may seem.

As you go through this process, you will start to realize that the path you have chosen widely varies from the mainstream population, the Sheep. Your confidence will soar, and self-esteem will be pure and hardened. You may actually start to think you are better than other people, walking on water.

Well, hold your horses right there. No human being is better than any other human being; we are all born equally with our God-given inner potential. It's just that some take a different approach to life. This makes you different, not better. View your newfound worthiness as a tool to bring others along with you for the climb. One of your core principles should be aligned with compassion. You have an obligation to lift those less fortunate *who want to be lifted* – and note this is one reason you cannot rescue a Snake. They have no wish to be saved. But if others want to be helped and are receptive to your guidance, you can have influence on the lives of others. Remember, teach what you learn.

> *"Be brave enough to go after what you really want.*
> *Be strong enough to pick people up and bring them with you."*
> --Andy Frisella

CHAPTER SIXTEEN

A LITTLE KNOWLEDGE GOES A LONG WAY!

Who is writing\ the chapters of your life?

As you know, I am a huge advocate of applying common sense to your daily life and not overthinking things so much. Developing common sense comes from your daily observations and your experiences of how the life machine operates. This requires being receptive and open-minded, which in turn means you are consistently and proactively gaining knowledge. You should always be engaged and develop a habit of looking for micro-strategic advantages. This chapter covers some of the content that I used to teach at my companies over the years to help you start to gain your perspective of not only seeking knowledge but how to retain and apply it in your daily life:

As mentioned in the introduction, there is no better understanding of the game of winning in life than Tim Grover's book *Winning*. Winning in life is the accumulation of wins over decades of effort in all areas of the five horizons that I will cover in the "ladder" chapters. Winning consistently over a lifetime is a requirement to reach the top rungs of your ladder where serenity awaits.

Winning a game, a championship, a big contract, or the person of your dreams are only individual rungs up the ladder that must be repeated and duplicated to reach that serenity. This concept of winning has no destination; it lasts for eternity and goes to the grave with you. There is no retirement from winning; only the playing field changes over time.

Hence, you need to keep the wins coming. For me, winning transformed into more things of value as I have gotten older, like physical challenges, relationships, writing this book, caring for my elderly parents, and making my wife the happiest woman on the planet. With every win your immediate thought should be, "Next!"

The faith factor of winning
You do not live in the moment...you live for the moment

> "I trained four years to run nine seconds."
> --Usain Bolt

When we set out to accomplish anything, we visualize the win in some form. How you see it from the onset is critically important to the outcome. The history of your efforts will determine your growth and future wins.

My youngest daughter is a competitive acrobat. Last season, her trio launched with a first-place finish in the opening season competition. They won the second competition and then the third. They qualified for the USA Nationals in Tulsa, Oklahoma, and entered the field of the nation's best 25 teams undefeated. They gave a stellar performance under the most pressured circumstances and ended up winning the National Championship with a score of 51.70. The second-place team totaled 51.65. This is a win by .05-tenths of a point.

What was the difference that caused one team to edge out the other by the narrowest of margins? One extra Sunday practice? Better coaching? Was it our exceptional tumbler, doing homework in the car to fit in all the hours? Could it have been choreography? The diet and nutrition of the athletes? Was it the extra conditioning after practices? Was it the leadership and camaraderie of the three girls? This list could go on for hundreds of reasons why one team wins, and another loses even by the narrowest of margins, but the answer to the question is *all of the above.*

You practice, rehearse, and repeat…not to get it right, but until you can't get it wrong.

> *"Vision without execution is hallucination."*
> --Thomas Edison

It's in the details of hundreds or thousands of little efforts that make the difference and having the faith to execute all of them. You will never know which one pushed you over your competition, which is why a relentless effort in all areas of life is required 24/7 to win all meaningful championships. This is the only path to victory in the ultimate game called life.

These girls got their first experience as Falcons as the precision of their routine was built on the *details* of their execution. Their floor routine was perfectly synchronized, and the skills were executed to perfection. When you are "all in," you will build an unwavering faith: "If I work long and hard enough and do everything within my power to succeed, I tilt the odds in my favor." This is the same process that led me to my bodybuilding championship. Life is about consistently positioning yourself for the win to maximize your potential to get the win.

Many people who think they are "all in" have not scratched the surface of what the real commitment needs to be.

There are no guarantees of winning, no matter how concerted the effort, but an "all in" effort that does not produce a win at the moment is *still* a win in process, and will contribute to future potential wins.

As we already know, life is simply a game of odds and percentages, so why not tilt those percentages in your favor with everything you approach in life? Although it took me a lifetime to learn how to win at one thing, winning for me is not the championship anymore. Now, it's the resilience to come back repeatedly, whether there is a victory or defeat. This is serenity.

Ask that question, make that call

There are two facets to this lesson.

<u>Stronger Communication</u>

The first is simply a matter of communication. As most of us know, in today's world, because of texts, emails, and instant messaging, communication suffers. People don't talk to each other like they used to. This causes a level of insecurity when communication directly by phone or in person becomes necessary. My salespeople wanted to communicate by text or email; they weren't eager to pick up the phone.

Yes, there are places and times when quick, efficient messaging or email is the better option. From a business perspective, it is usually best to communicate in the manner that the customer prefers. But when you have an issue, a disagreement, or a misunderstanding, it won't likely be resolved through text or email. In fact, you're probably going to make it worse. The way people convey themselves in those short messages removes the human, emotional component. Our perception of the conversation can become skewed. I emphasized to my salespeople, "Ask whatever it is you don't know. Make the call first."

More than 90% of sales transactions are resolved in live communication, meaning with a call, a Zoom, or a face-to-face meeting.

When you make a phone call, there is a conversation. Whatever the conclusion is, it is resolved because we interact with each other in real time. When you send an email on a controversial issue or a disagreement, it could be 24 hours or more before a response comes. It may not come at all if your email went into their spam – this means you wait, and the other person has plenty of time to misconstrue your meaning. There's doubt on both sides. It causes a lot of unwarranted stress, not to mention lack of efficiency.

I'm about resolving things as quickly and efficiently as possible. Whatever people may call their success, they still have problems they need to resolve, and the better a person is at solutions, the more productive and content they will be.

Essential knowledge

The second facet of "ask that question, make that call," is about our own resistance to asking questions about things we don't know or understand. We're so afraid of looking dumb or embarrassing ourselves in front of others that we'd rather go on in ignorance. We may also be afraid we won't like the answers we get, that we'll have to deal with negativity, that we might end up with even more work to do, or that we'll look unprofessional in front of others.

But we have to admit this: ignorance is a huge risk. Don't ever think that the old saying, "Ignorance is bliss" has any validity. Ignorance is one thing: stupidity! Even more embarrassing than "asking the obvious question" is later getting something wrong and having everyone guess – correctly – that you were just afraid to ask. But moving forward in ignorance can be more than humiliating. It can be risky and destructive, meaning the difference between success and failure.

One final, critical thing to remember about communication: you never know to whom you are talking. Treat every contact or customer like they are your path to $100 million!

Always ask because the worst thing you can hear is "no."

We have a terrible fear of rejection. But since life is a game of odds and percentages, the chances of getting something without asking are zero. Even a one-in-a-million chance is better odds than not asking.

I had tremendous success at an early age just by asking for things I needed.

I had no money as a kid. I was twelve years old and fell in love with golf. But I had no way to pay to practice or play. Golf is expensive, especially for a kid. I would ride my bike up to the University of Maryland and practice around the putting greens. That didn't cost anything. But if you want to get a bucket of range balls or play on the course, there was a price. I tried to figure out a way to play and practice despite my lack of funds. One day, I went up to one of the pros at the club, Randy Hoffman, and I admit, I was terrified. But I said, "Mr. Hoffman, I'd really like to figure out a way I can practice a little more. Is there anything I can do around here to help out so I can get some free-range balls?"

He was immediately receptive to the idea, leading me further into a passion for golf that changed the course of my life. If I hadn't asked the question, who knows what would have happened? He arranged for me to come in with the driving range manager on Saturday and Sunday mornings at 7:00 am and pick up the golf balls around the outside of the fence. In exchange for that, he let me practice. Then it went from practice to playing, getting to know others, and making connections, and soon I had a regular job at the club. Little did I know that, six years later, he would be my coach when I played on the University of MD golf team.

Overcoming fear of asking

Asking questions can be uncomfortable. Whether asking about a concept you don't understand, asking teammates their opinion about a strategy, or asking for help, advice, a raise or a promotion, here are tips for conquering your fear of asking.

1. **Remember your overall objective while asking**. This will embolden you but also ensure that you're asking the right questions. You are solving a problem; ask the question that will provide the solution or a path to the solution.

2. **Focus on the benefits of the response.** Whether its increased understanding, or increased opportunities, you have much to gain by asking. Asking questions gains trust, too. When people believe you are interested in what they have to say, they like you more and are more inclined to help.

3. **Imagine what might go wrong** or get worse if you *don't* ask.

4. **Think of asking questions as a chance to get a new outlook.** If you fear answers that challenge your viewpoint, you'll never grow.

5. **Ask the right people at the right time.** This requires a bit of common-sense practice. Don't ask personal questions in public, for example. Don't interrupt a meeting with a question about a different project. Don't pressure someone to speak with you when they are obviously preoccupied or in a hurry. This is just tact. Approaching people at the right time can make the difference between yes and no.

6. **Be prepared for "no."** – Whenever you hear "no," you are one step closer to "yes." What's the backup game plan for "no?" When you hear "no," it is never over. It's just an opportunity to reassess, adjust, and ask again and again and again! When you tell a five-year-old she can't have that piece of candy, how many times will she ask again? 10, 15, 20 times? Who usually wins? This is what makes children the greatest salespeople of all!

Big fish and little fish

Talent wasted is a terrible burden to grow old with.

Everybody wants to be the biggest fish in the room because it's the most comfortable place to be. But if you ever want to grow, you need to be the smallest fish in the room, seeking advice and learning from the smarter, more experienced people around you.

Many of us feel nervous about seeking advice from those "big fish." We may view them as too important or too smart to have time for us. I recommend getting over this unfounded fear as quickly as possible. Don't view successful people as unapproachable; view successful people as "people" – that is the only way you can get comfortable putting yourself among those at the next level and getting somewhere.

I remember, as a young man, going to a business conference of entrepreneurs. I was terrified, as I had just started my first business and had little experience. I remember thinking, "I don't belong here. How do I introduce myself? What if someone asks me a question that I don't know the answer to? Am I wearing the right clothes?"

About thirty people showed up, and it was more of a social networking event, which made this even worse for me. I stayed for only about a half hour, speaking to no one. Initially I thought nothing great came from over this terrifying experience, but years later I realized that after that event I read a book on networking. I learned how to introduce myself, ask questions, and engage others. The lesson learned here: always show up. I didn't know it at the time, but without speaking to anyone, it was my first step in building relationships!

Allies versus friends

"Never tell your problems to anyone. 20% don't care,
and the other 80% are glad you have them."
--Lou Holtz

What's the difference between an ally and a friend? Friends are there for you if it's convenient. Allies will stand by you in tough times. Yes, a person can be both, but if a friend is not also an ally, it becomes quickly apparent. Are you attracted to purpose people or pleasure people? You need to choose one or the other. Purpose people have allies, not friends.

The only way that you will avoid the trap of a negative path is to get away from others who are going down that path. Associate with people who are like-minded, looking to go down a path of achievement, people who are there to support and help you, and likewise, for you to support and help them.

My youngest daughter is sixteen. She attends school in a world that's very different from what my older children experienced. She only has a couple of close, quality friends. She's not interested in hanging out or parties. I emphasized repeatedly, "This is the way life is going to go. You want to associate with people who want to do remarkable things and are mature beyond their years. As you get older, you have to stay away from people heading down destructive paths." I'm really proud of her. In high school, there is so much peer pressure. A high percentage of the kids are headed down the wrong path. It takes a lot of self-esteem, a good self-concept, and confidence to go this direction when we're young. By skipping the party years, you can launch yourself years ahead of the Sheep and climb your ladders with fewer setbacks. Though it is a difficult concept, it is sometimes necessary to remove people from our lives. And sometimes, that can even include siblings, parents, and other relatives. You don't have to actually eliminate them from your life, of course; I would never suggest cutting ties with one's family except in extreme cases, but you do have to learn to accept them for who they are, contain them in a place that's not destructive, and then choose your own path if theirs is not aligned with yours.

Most people are all about balance, low stress and the path of least resistance. For me, that is a potential path of regret. As you age, you begin to think of all the things you wished you would have done...but anything you wished you had done would have taken some obsessive behavior if you want to excel to a level of high achievement and get it done. Your true allies will be joyful and supportive of your success. Since only the Cheetahs, Falcons, and Lions think this way, this could be a very lonely place from time to time.

What you don't know can only help you!
  Knowledge gained without experience can be dangerous.

It is often said there are three levels of knowledge:
- What you know
- What you don't know
- What you don't know that you don't know. Most knowledge is right here, in this void of everything we've never been exposed to. Once we understand how very much, we have to learn, we open ourselves up to a universe of new understanding.

When we're young, we have big dreams about the possibilities in life. We imagine we could be spies, astronauts, rock stars, sports stars, movie directors, showbiz celebrities, or CEOs of world-changing companies. Every kid in Little League can see the Major Leagues in their future. This is not a bad thing; it's just that, as kids, we don't have a concept of what we're up against. We don't know the vastness of the odds that are against them. But what we don't know only helps us at that point because we are willing to relentlessly pursue that near-impossible dream.

We may grow out of dreams of being the next Patrick Mahomes or Taylor Swift, but even as adults, we still have that spark of the "impossible dream" lighting us deep down inside. I might launch into an entrepreneurial endeavor with my hopes high, believing the sky is the limit. But do I really understand that 90% of new businesses fail, or that I'm committing myself to working 100+ hours a week, or that I will spend many sleepless nights worrying about where the next customer will come from? Probably not. If we really believed in those odds, few of us would put ourselves through the wringer like that. There would be no new business at all!

Our faith that we can succeed despite the odds is a good thing – because if we didn't have it, we'd never try.

When my son Justin played hockey, he and the other teens on his team all believed that their skill sets were elite enough to take them "all the way." Their beliefs weren't completely unfounded, either. This wasn't a pee-wee league. These kids were talented players in high-level competition for their age group. But of all the kids my son played with, over many years, we know one who actually made it to the NHL – and that in itself is remarkable. My son loved hockey. He was early to practice, extremely coachable, always ready and willing to help out the coach and team. He did all the off-ice training. He was in the gym five days a week, building up his muscle mass. Over five or six years of significant effort, there came a time when an elite former NHL all-star coach said, "Son, you need to go play for a college team. You're not going to make it to the next level."

At this point, my son could have been devastated. A lot of young people would have been. But he looked at this situation practically, saying, "I did everything I could to get there. If I didn't make it, I can live with that."

There is no shame in getting knocked out. The shame is not getting in the ring!

The real regret, you see, would have been in never knowing how far he could have gone if he had *really* tried or been "all in." I lived through that myself, never knowing just how good I could have been at golf if I'd done the things I really needed to do. I quit, and so I'll always wonder.

When you pursue something at a high level and give it your all – if ultimately you don't make it, you still have the solid experience, training, and knowledge that it took to get that far. And that's not for nothing. It's still a win in its own perspective. If you approach a horizon and go farther than everyone else, it will translate to every other aspect of your life. 99% of us may not achieve that elusive childhood dream, but we learn the process of success that launches us to other endeavors.

Unanswered Prayers

> *"…just because He doesn't answer, doesn't mean He don't care*
> *'Cause some of God's greatest gifts are unanswered prayers."*
> --Garth Brooks, "Unanswered Prayers"

So many times, we believe we want something. We strive for it with everything we have. We don't believe our lives can be complete without it. And still, it doesn't happen. The loss of that person, that opportunity, that goal, seems like the worst thing that could happen. We may grieve for it for a long time.

But eventually, in hindsight, we see that what we wanted wasn't as great as we believed. Without that loss, we wouldn't be the people we are now. We might even be relieved to see that our lives went in a different direction. "I'm so glad I didn't go down that path!" we say. Or we may think, "Wow, I really dodged a bullet there!"

This happens frequently with romance, and the people whom we become infatuated with. We are certain our lives will be incomplete without them. Yet relationships based on the shaky grounds of infatuation often fail, and we suffer devastation. Yet how often do we look back at those old relationships and see what a disaster it might have been? "What was I thinking? Things would never have worked out between us."

When we don't get the things that we want, it's not always a bad thing. A young man's heart might be set on playing football for a certain college, but they cut him. He thinks his dreams are over and, dejectedly, takes his chances at another college, someplace he never thought he'd wind up. There, maybe he finds a great coach and a different opportunity, and he becomes a superstar. Or maybe he learns something else about himself – that his real talent lies elsewhere, leading him down the path to a brilliant career. The point is, if he'd gotten what he thought he really wanted, he would never have moved into this amazing new world.

We all have the ability to say, "If that thing hadn't happened, I wouldn't have what I have now." Regardless of how badly we think we want something, nothing is all-encompassing. Young people have a lot of trouble with this concept, usually just because their experience is so limited that they don't know the scope of possibilities. Adults, too, can be trapped by their circumstances and unable to see beyond the imaginary walls we bind ourselves in.

Question everything

> *"The highest form of ignorance is to reject*
> *something you know nothing about."*
> --Wayne Dyer

Most of who we are, what we are, and what we learn is a result of who we are around: our parents, family, those who are closest to us. The irony is sometimes that the people closest to us are in "protection mode." They don't want to see us get hurt, or see anything negative happen to us. There's always an air of caution when we get advice from people who love us because they are risk-averse.

Directly opposite this is the strong influence of bullshit social media, where we can sit all day hearing a vast variety of useless information, vitriol advice with nothing solid backing it up. In fact, most of it is a scam.

We are always drawn to and ready to believe what we have been programmed to believe. We repeatedly tell lies to ourselves due to misinformation.

Therefore, one of the keys to being super-successful is to question everything we have been taught to believe. "I've always thought this… but wait a second. Maybe I can look at it in a different way."

Another effective way to look at this is a habit we can find in great leaders.

Joe Gibbs was the head coach of the Washington Redskins during a phenomenal decade for the team, back in the 1980s and early 1990s. He often brought in coaches with different strategies and philosophies because he was open-minded to new viewpoints.

Great presidents in the past were willing to do the same. They didn't surround themselves with an inner circle who all thought the same way but with people who disagreed with them and offered up different viewpoints.

It has taken me many years to understand this, but now I know even someone I adamantly disagree with may have something to teach me.

Question everything. We are so ingrained in habit that, at some point, we have to question things in order to push forward. The investing world is a notable example of this. We're taught to put money in a 401(k), work 40 years and hopefully have enough money to retire and take a vacation now and then. That's ridiculous. We have to say, "Maybe that's not for me. What if I don't want to get wealthy over 40 years? What if I want to get rich in five years? Who has done that?" Lots of people have done that. Those are the ones we should look at. Question the status quo of things in life. If the Sheep are doing it, you shouldn't!

Work on yourself first

"People are attracted to people who make themselves a priority."
--Brad Lea

The tact of working on yourself first may seem counterintuitive, and many people never fully understand this. We wake each day with responsibilities: career, family, social obligations, faith…all these things that are part of our lives. Most people forget that if they take better care of themselves, they will be better at all these obligations.

Self-care means many things. Health and fitness, mental capacity, self-education, and all the things you spend time on for yourself. I used to believe that I could never miss one of my kids' games. And I did make that work. But do we have to be at every single event, if there are other obligations that will make us better parents in other capacities? There is a common guilty trope we have in society now, that missing any of our children's "moments" will crush them as individuals. This is simply not true. We have to put ourselves first sometimes, creating a better image of ourselves, improving our self-esteem, and creating a level of respect. Sometimes, we have a decision to make: what is really best for the family?

We can become embroiled in the emotional side of our life instead of understanding that the emotional path is not always the wisest one. Children are resilient and respect a parent who meets obligations. Remember, our children are observers of *us* and will observe what we *do* far more than what we say or preach to them. Kids are smart as hell, and they pick up on everything. Our leadership roles have a huge influence on them. If they see fundamental leadership of a family in how their parents engage and work for the good of the family, they will respond positively to that with respect.

Trust Yourself

"If you are broke, it is not your fault.
If you die broke, it's 100% your fault."
--J.T. Foxx

I have lived most of my life in defiance of what other people thought; I always had the ability to question everything. If I made a poor decision, I would much rather suffer the results of my poor decisions than the results of someone else's poor decisions. Most people are in the second category, a victim of other people's choices.

I disagreed with my father on most things related to business and finances because he was conservative, low-key, and avoided conflict. He was an extremely successful small businessperson, but he was not a confrontational personality. I was the opposite of that, ready to argue and defy authority. I found, as life went on, and I listened to advice from other people, that my own intuition and thoughts were right most of the time.

The only way we learn to trust ourselves is to make tough decisions. If we're wrong, we're wrong – but if we rely on others to make our decisions and go against our own beliefs, we do ourselves an injustice. I was often told when I was younger that I was "wrong." Society, school especially, kept implying to me that I was unable to learn, that I wasn't as smart as the other kids. This ruffled my feathers, you might say. Subconsciously, I thought, "I'll show them. I'll prove them wrong about me."

My self-esteem demanded that I trust myself from an early age. Whatever I chose to do, I did it to the extreme. I sought to be the best at everything I did; that's why team sports didn't appeal to me. The other kids weren't as invested; they didn't care as much as I cared about winning, so it's no wonder I ended up in the golf arena. Me against me!

Exceed your own expectations

*"Your obligation to yourself must be greater
than obligations put on you by others."*
--Tim Grover

Everyone has expectations for us. I've learned a little trick over the years that has served me very well: Set and exceed my own expectations, which, in every case, exceeds the expectations of others. No one can know what you are capable of but you. Build that inner fire that says, "Fuck you, world! I got this."

I don't discuss my internal expectations with anyone, I diligently, quietly, and simply execute them. I don't need anyone's approval or congratulations as the internal contentment drives me to what's next, next, and next. I just let them see the results and watch them wonder, "Why is he always winning?" Try this for yourself. Internalize a difficult goal, tell no one, and go get it!

You won't need to tell anyone. They'll know!

When you do one thing really well, and you put your blood, sweat, tears, and pain into it, it changes your perspective forever. Few people do that. But knowing you have accomplished this incredible thing puts you in an amazing place. Conquering multiple challenges and piling up the wins has changed me forever! My view of life and my perspective is in an extremely good place here at age 64 – far better than it was when I was 40 and better than I could have ever imagined. A lot of that comes down to my personal expectations and accountability to myself.

Strategic Advantage

Most of the time, when you hear the phrase "strategic advantage" or "competitive advantage," it's related to business practices or sports. As I mentioned before, I would like you to think of yourself as a brand or a business. If you were your own brand, wouldn't you want to search for every opportunity to get better, build your brand, and become a juggernaut in the market? If you were an Olympic athlete, wouldn't you want to refine every detail to optimize performance? This can be achieved by consistently searching for your competitive and strategic advantages. I want to win at all the little things!

Strategic advantage is a mindset that evolves into daily habitual actions. A good bit of this comes from "The Great Observer" chapter: awareness and clear vision of your surroundings to seek out opportunity to take actions others miss or ignore. I like to think of gaining a strategic advantage as a competition: me versus the world on a daily basis. Where can I perform better to be more efficient, more productive and execute at a higher level than anyone else?

I particularly pay attention to seeking ways to compress my time. You may have seen my vacation videos of business trips when I go to the gym at 6:00 am. I may be in a resort or hotel of several hundred people, yet I'll be alone, the only one in the gym. This is a clear strategic advantage. Most people are hungover, ate too much the night before, or are just too damn lazy to get their asses out of bed. I like to do what others are not willing to do. I do daily what everyone else does occasionally. Regimented daily disciplines make you more efficient and therefore compress the time it takes to climb your ladder. Strategic advantages will boost your confidence and evolve into creative, innovative thinking.

There has never been a better time to execute on the concept of a strategic advantage. Right now, society as a whole is lazy, entitled, and uneducated. Few people have any idea how to build an exceptional life up the ladder or a willingness to do the work. Because of this, the opportunity to gain your strategic advantages and accelerate your life is a wide-open highway without traffic!

David Goggins calls it "front-loading your life." Devour everything right now because no one else is hungry.

Be prepared for the haters:

> *"Mediocre people don't like high achievers,*
> *and high achievers don't like mediocre people."*
> --Nick Saban

Throughout human history, Sheep have envied the Cheetahs, Falcons, and Alpha Lions. This is more evident in today's divisive society than it has ever been. Like I said earlier, what part of what I earned are you entitled to? Referring back to our chapter on human nature, this is a natural process of human behavior. Since the majority of people have never been in the trenches, strived for excellence, or excelled at an impossible endeavor, most of those people live in a world of ignorance about the Cheetah's lifestyle.

Therefore, we cannot blame the sheep for their attacks on our success, but we can expect it. Envy is a normal human emotion. Sheep are victims of their complacency and mediocre lifestyle, whereas the Cheetahs are victors, evolving from their 100% accountability for their own outcomes. As a Cheetah climbs the ladder, it can anticipate that it will get resistance from its circle of friends and even its family.

Remember, we only associate with allies, so as you grow, the friends must go. You will be criticized and ridiculed, and people may think you have lost your mind as you excel in your new world of exceptionalism. Now here's the ironic part: you *want* haters! The more successful you are, the more you will discover people who can't handle the new you. Allies will cheer for your success, while the Sheep envy your success. As you develop more haters, it's a direct sign of your development, growth, and advancement up the ladder.

How you manage your haters is critically important. You must use them as an asset. First, never respond to a hater. You cannot win a battle with ignorance. This is especially true on social media. Furthermore, you cannot refute lies from what appear to be credible sources. Secondly, use the haters as fuel that confirms you are on the right path to becoming a Cheetah. And lastly and most important, never cave to a hater. Do not change your stance, outlook, or responses because someone does not like the new you!

Remember, your developed inner moral core of resilience should guide you through any issues with the haters. Stand by your principles and do not compromise your ethics or beliefs for anyone or anything.

"Never cater to a hater, just say 'Later!'"
--Vanilla Ice

Life will throw you curve balls, changeups,
and every now and then, blow a fast ball right by you.
It's not the last "out" you made,
but how you approach your next at-bat
that determines your fortune and quality of life.

CHAPTER SEVENTEEN

THE LADDER PREPARATION

"The graveyard is the richest place on earth because it is here that
you will find all the hopes and dreams that were never fulfilled,
the books that were never written, the songs that were never sung,
the inventions that were never shared, the cures that were never
discovered, all because someone was too afraid to take that
first step, keep with the problem, or determined
to carry out their dream."
- Les Brown

Once you have established your solid foundation for launch discussed in chapter 2, it's time to begin moving up your ladder rung by rung. This process requires an understanding of a few key components that will enable you to execute in a consistent manner.

Climbing your ladder is a lifestyle. It's not a some-of-the-time thing or change here and there. It's a slow transition, programming your mind to be in winning mode the majority of the time. As we start this process, there are four key concepts that will require you to develop deep commitment to these principles: Mindset, Everything Counts, Efficiency, and Logic Over Emotion.

Mindset

"When you do more than you're paid to do,
you will eventually be paid more for what you do."
--Zig Ziglar

Get your hands dirty!

Here is a simple story with enormous impact and many lessons. When I was sixteen, I worked at the University of Maryland's golf course driving range. When the range closed each evening at 10 pm, it was the night shift's job to pick up all the balls with the tractor, so the ball bin was full and ready for the morning shift.

We worked in shifts of two. The junior worker, which was me, had the job of taking out the tractor and picking up all the balls. This was about an hour-long process. On this particular evening, when I went to pull the tractor out of the parking area, the rack that held the steel ball picker had somehow broken off and separated from the tractor. My immediate response was this was great news - I could get off work early that night!

I was working that evening with one of the more senior guys whose name was Mark. So, when I walked back to the sales shack excited to tell Mark what happened, and that we could wrap it up early, he said to me, "Let me see your hands."

I had no idea what he was talking about, but I showed them to him with curiosity. He then pointed to the tool repair box and said firmly to me, "Get back out there, and come back when your hands are dirty."

I knew exactly what he meant, so off I went with a poor attitude to try to repair the tractor. After about 15 minutes of inspection, I discovered that the shear pin where the rack attached to the tractor had broken off. Sure enough, when I opened the toolbox, there were several replacement pins at the top of the toolbox, plus all of the tools I needed to do the repair.

It took me about 30 minutes to figure out how to use all the tools I needed and to build supports under the rack to hold it while I replaced the shear pin. The total process took about an hour, and when it was completed, I looked down, and my hands were dirty and greasy. When I proudly returned to tell Mark it was fixed, he simply smiled and went about his business.

The simple lesson Mark taught me was invaluable to my future. It immediately boosted my self-esteem and confidence. Prior to that experience, I mostly had a fixed mindset. Not only was it my view that this was someone else's job, I considered it someone else's problem. I was also preprogrammed to believe that I could not do it because it never crossed my mind to even try. The experience taught me what a growth mindset was and to always leave things better than I found them.

From that day forward, I embraced every challenge. This experience served me well when starting my first business.

What a great lesson for a 16-year-old. Mark, if you are out there, here is a "thank you!" well overdue.

I'll now give you another must-read book: Carol Dweck's *Mindset*. As you dig into this invaluable content, you will discover that your mindset has everything to do with your path in life and your climb up the ladder. Mindset is a mental attitude or inclination. Do you have a fixed mindset or a growth mindset? Do you have the ability to consistently move from a doubter to a believer? People with a fixed mindset live in a victimized state whereby they think the world and outside circumstances dictate their destiny. They also view their potential as predetermined. All Sloths and most Sheep have a fixed mindset.

People with a growth mindset live in a victor state whereby they believe they are personally in control of their destiny. Cheetahs live in this world. Folks with a growth mindset use failure as a launching pad to expand their minds, develop intelligence, and climb to the next level. In every failure, there is something to be gained, whereas those with a fixed mindset will forever be in the "woe is me" state of mind. The difference will affect every decision you make. Mistakes don't define you; they refine you. Having a development mindset will keep you challenged over and over again, which in turn will keep your mind wondering and curious about all the possibilities in front of you. Your attitude determines your altitude!

Children who are taught growth mindset principles by teachers, coaches, and parents actually develop higher IQs, as their minds are filled with evolving perceptions and they are constantly challenged by new endeavors.

Everything counts

Are you driven by purpose and duty or pleasure and desire?

Back in 1991, Brian Tracy published the audio program, *The Universal Laws of Success and Achievement.*

Although this title seems to go against my "no rules, no laws" guideline, I recommend you download this audiobook, as its content is exceptional. One of the best lessons I derived from it was the belief that "Everything Counts." Every thought, every action, and every non-action has, in some way, an impact on your life and your future. Therefore, everything you think, say, and do propels you one rung up your ladder or drives you one rung down.

There is no neutrality in business, relationships, or in life. When trying to keep the status quo, you lose ground because your environment and surrounding world are moving rapidly. This is clearly noted in the business world, where companies that rely on their past successes and rest on their laurels are quickly eaten alive by the companies that are in constant innovation and growth. These business owners wake up one day in bankruptcy court wondering, "What happened?"

The world is a "take it to it" place, not a "bring it to me" place. There is no clearer example than Blockbuster video, which rented VHS tapes, and later, DVDs of movies. As technology evolved, they failed to evolve alongside it, and what was once a thriving mega million-dollar business quickly became obsolete and went bankrupt. On the other hand, Netflix did the opposite and evolved from a mail order DVD rental platform to the juggernaut streaming giant they are today.

View your life in this exact same manner. Who you are today will be obsolete tomorrow. By constantly reinventing yourself, you will remain relevant not only in your career but in your relationships as well.

My wife and I thrive on our personal growth and push each other to new heights, both physically and mentally. We want to look good for each other as well as remain interesting and relevant in an ever-changing world. This is how we grow together, and we know that life's next step for us is always optimistic. We wake up as a team every day like we are just getting started! Our goals are simple: recognize that everything counts and move one rung up our ladder as often as possible. I should also note that by being the best we can be for each other with an innovative mindset keeps the fire burning in our marriage and enables us to fall more in love year after year. It's a wonderful place to be, and you can get there too!

The concept of everything counts requires taking inventory of your actions. This works in all time frames, whether by the minute or hour, daily, weekly, monthly, or yearly. For the purpose of simplifying the process and gaining maximum impact, let's focus on your daily inventory. At the end of each day, you either moved up one rung on your ladder or down one rung. Remember, there is no neutrality in life. Creating and accumulating micro-wins throughout the day will send you up a rung when you take inventory at the end of the day.

For most people, this focus on collecting and inventorying micro-wins will require some discipline to change any daily habits that have kept you in a place of neutrality or complacency.

The question is, "Did I move one step closer to my positive goals and visions through the actions I took today?" This applies to all areas of life, from health and wellness, career, relationships, parenting, long-term goals, and so on. To simplify this concept, let's say you know you need to lose 20 pounds. Your energy is low, you feel sluggish, and you decide it's time to make a change. You think of all the things you need to do to lose 20 lbs., like joining a gym, eating a clean diet, eliminating the two alcoholic drinks each evening, skipping happy hour on Fridays, passing the convenience stores, and cutting out the casual drug use on the weekends. Your awareness of these necessities, and any action or non-action that avoids those necessities, creates a loss every day. The rungs of the ladder began to slip from beneath you, and the growing ladder above you gets steeper with each daily loss. The climb back up grows tougher and tougher.

On the other hand, perhaps you take action, hire a personal trainer, get a daily regimen started of diet and exercise, toss out the alcohol at your house, and wake up an hour earlier each day. This will immediately lead to daily wins, and you will begin to scale up your ladder. *Everything counts.*

First and foremost, you must recognize and understand the concept so you can immediately take action and move up some rungs in the right direction. Was today's inventory a win or a loss? Tomorrow is a new day!

> *"You cannot escape the responsibility of tomorrow by evading it today."*
> --Abraham Lincoln

Become an efficiency freak
Slow down and smell the roses?
How about speed up and own the entire rose farm?

Time is your most precious commodity. If you doubt this, I challenge you to ask one hundred 70-year-olds what's the most important thing to treasure in life. The overall response will be time and what they did with it. In order to scale up your ladder at a faster pace, it's important to understand this concept at an early age. Procrastination, excuses, and dead, unplanned casual time will eventually catch up to you. The longer you delay engaging in your personal battle for success, the more difficult the battle and the associated climb will be later. Develop an efficient, do-it-now attitude at once. Yesterday is gone, and it's not coming back. If you live to 90 years old, that's only 32,850 days. That will give you some perspective on the importance of every hour of every day in starting now to build an exceptional life.

Just like so many other concepts in this book, you need to develop an awareness of becoming super-efficient. **How you do one thing is how you do everything!** Pay attention to details where you waste precious time in your daily routine. Do you hit your alarm's snooze button over and over? Is your shower 30 minutes long? Do you check driving routes for traffic before leaving? Being organized and developing regimented routines creates efficiency. Yes, you will have to do things differently than the average Sheep.

For example, almost no one answers their phone if they do not recognize the number or know the contact. If it turns out that you needed to take that call, this creates a voicemail. You then have to check the voicemail and return the call, and then you may need to leave a voicemail as well. These simple inefficiencies throughout your day not only rob you of your time but create unnecessary stress.

Another part of being an efficiency freak is resolving all tasks and concerns immediately. Return all texts and emails immediately or as soon as you can physically get to them. Develop the habit of being in attack mode for all tasks. Leaving work for later, especially if it's related to a problem that needs to be resolved, creates anxiety and will affect your other activities as well. Keep your plate empty as efficiently as possible.

Some of you may immediately think that this is a stressful lifestyle, but it's actually the opposite. Having outstanding work and tasks building up to be overwhelming is stressful, not efficiently working them as they come about. You will boost your self-esteem and operate in auto mode as your approach to efficiency develops. This habit is a key characteristic of high achievers.

We all remember putting off our homework after school for the instant gratification of recreational time. The entire time you were playing, you were stressed because you knew that later that evening, the work had to be done. On the other hand, there were times when you immediately executed your homework right after school and had the joyful feeling all evening of some recreational time without the stress. The Cheetah is hungry and keeps his plate clean as often as possible. He takes on the tough stuff first. This simple example defines the efficiency of the Cheetah's path up the ladder!

When my youngest son was pitching in college, he had an injury to his UCL and needed Tommy John surgery. We had a contact that got us in to see the famous surgeon who invented the surgery and had performed it on many major league players. We had a date for the surgery with Dr. James Andrews at his complex in Pensacola, Florida. When we arrived, the facilities were impressive, with multiple buildings, including the surgery center, research center, and a full rehab center. It was quite an expansive campus. Dr. Andrews did anywhere from 4-7 surgeries daily. My son was on the schedule for an early slot at 7 am.

When we were in the prep area, I read a framed newspaper article on the wall. The reporter asked Dr. Andrews how he managed all of his responsibilities and ran such a large medical operation, as well as being a team doctor for the NFL. The response was one line: "I answer my phone." The point was, he managed himself professionally and efficiently. With his schedule, he could not afford to have backlogs on his planner and 20 voicemails to return. High performers take care of things *now*.

Patience versus Duration

"Patience is a virtue." "Everything comes to those who wait." We have all heard these old sayings. But when time is your most precious commodity, why do you want to wait for anything?

Understanding the difference between patience and duration is important. There are many things about life that take a long time. Most success takes a lengthy time of duration.

However, there is a significant difference between duration and patience. All high-level winners use a concept where they compress time, which in turn compresses the duration. You don't want to be patient about anything, you want to be an efficiency freak.

Let me simplify this for you. If you are out on a casual bike ride and you approach a short but steep hill, what's your mindset? Do you be patient, shift down to first gear, and slowly work your way up the hill for three minutes? Or do you get up out of the saddle, stay in third gear, attack that hill, and summit it in one minute? Both options require some pain and suffering, but the second option shortens the time frame of pain and suffering and shortens your duration.

Now you know the mentality of all elite achievers; however, 90% of you will choose option one, the slower, patient approach, even though enduring more pain and suffering for shorter periods of time will lead to more moments of contentment and euphoria in your life.

Just imagine applying this principle to your finances. Do you want to be a millionaire in 50 years or 5 years? I don't know about you, but time is all I've got. I want to get everything I want out of life as soon and efficiently as possible. Understand your duration, but remember there is no need to be patient in your approach to anything! Stop analyzing and execute!

Being on time and ahead of time

I have heard and read so many times that you should not worry about being on time, that trying to be on time creates stress and can actually shorten your life.

This is a 100% Sheep mentality and the biggest crock of bullshit I have ever heard. If there is one thing you should do to create efficiencies in your life, it is to start showing up 15 minutes early to everything. When you prepare early, it gives you added relaxing time to address another short-term task. Being on time is the simplest form of reliability and accountability. If you can't do that or don't believe that, please enjoy your Sheep life to the best of your ability. Try showing up 10 minutes late to an NFL player meeting and see what happens. For that matter, try it at Apple or Microsoft and see what happens.

High-performing leaders have zero tolerance for mediocrity or complacency, and being efficient eliminates both of those characteristics. At my company, if you were not in the room when the meetings started without advance notice of why you were late, the door was closed, and you were not allowed to attend.

When my oldest son was moving up in leagues in hockey, trying to get to his aspiration of playing Division 1 hockey, we quickly discovered at the junior level, where they have their version of the Combine for hockey, that he simply did not have the size and speed to compete with the dominant kids at that level. Although he was a talented finesse player, he was not good enough to get looked at by D1 schools.

However, he was always the first one on the ice, always came to camps and practices in top condition, and he earned respect from his teammates and coaches due to his work ethic and reliability. Coaches loved him! I knew this mindset would serve him well, and sure enough, he made that junior team and did go on to play college hockey, although not D1. This didn't matter because the real win was his efficient, reliable attitude learned from sports that led him to an elite level of success in the business world.

Efficiency involves planning, and you need to make it a priority. I apply a lot of common sense to my approach here. If I have an hour's drive but know that traffic may be an issue, I'm leaving in time to give myself at least a 30-minute cushion. When everyone else is late due to traffic and you are on time, how does that look for you? Efficiencies create strategic advantages. You come across as a dependable person and the one who can be counted on. Remember, you want to create the aura of being the "go-to" person. The one that everyone can count on 100% of the time. You will also evolve to a higher level of respect. This is imperative not only in your professional life but in your personal life as well. My allies, business associates, and family know they count on me like the sun coming up tomorrow morning.

A fact/logic-based life vs. an opinion/emotional-based life.

"Your mind must be stronger than your feelings. Control your thoughts, and you'll control your emotions. Control your emotions, and you'll control your actions. Control your actions, you'll control the outcome."
--Tim Grover

Emotional intelligence is not what I am looking to eliminate from your life or thought process. Many of our emotions are of great benefit to our well-being, and in some ways, they create a balance in our life that is required to bring us back to an even playing field in our mind that's needed from time to time. We have six basic emotions: sadness, happiness, fear, anger, surprise, and disgust, and all are part of how we are made. It's in all of us. We are emotional animals by nature, but we have also been given the gift of logic, which enables choice.

When we look around, we see thousands of people living in a 100% emotional world that defies all logic. I am astonished to see so many people who are imprisoned by their emotions and therefore are a complete detriment to themselves and those around them. Men are typically logically strong but emotionally weak, whereas women are more likely to have strong intuitive emotions which at times can overshadow their logical thoughts. Awareness is the key.

I like to co-mingle logic with common sense, and from my perspective, with the observations of behavior I see daily, common sense has reached an all-time low in our society. The good news, this means more opportunities for you. It's just another area for you to gain a competitive edge and separate yourself from the Snakes and the Sheep of the world.

You should understand that logic is the language of the conscious mind; emotion is the language of the subconscious mind. Feelings lie; numbers and facts don't.

Have you ever wondered why you find yourself making the same mistakes or wrong decisions repeatedly? It's normal, and we all do it from time to time, but when it happens, we wonder ,*why do I keep doing that*? Furthermore, when this happens, we all tend to beat ourselves up about it as we know logically, we would not want to make the same mistakes repeatedly, yet it occurs anyway. Welcome to the world of your emotional brain. Approximately 70% of all decisions we make are based on emotion vs. logic.

Furthermore, a study performed by Nobel Prize-winning psychologist Daniel Kahneman said that we make financial decisions based 90% on emotion and only 10% on logic. So, in a world where our emotions will rule most of our decisions, even critical ones, how can we learn to change this behavior and move in a direction to build a life weighing in more fact and logic?

At some point, all high-level climbers up the ladder understand this concept and begin to work on the process of thought. The mindset to use a fact-based thought process is something that you need to develop over time. Yes, it will be a battle between your logical mind and your emotional mind. However, you get to determine the winner!

The first thing is simply to recognize and understand this concept. Try to catch yourself when you regret a decision or a behavior. Make a mental note: *I'm doing that differently next time.* The best way to practice is with short-term negative behaviors. Literally ask yourself, "Why did I just do that?" Be careful, because in the short term, this process can be portrayed in your mind as taking losses. However, as long as you know the long-term goal, that bad feeling when you recognize a negative emotional decision is just part of the process; it will register in your mind as progress and therefore a win.

This process takes years of conscious effort, but no matter how many times you repeat a negative-based emotional decision or behavior, keep working on it. You want to improve your mental process. It is very unlikely you will ever conquer it completely simply because of our human nature of being an emotional animal. But be aware of your emotions, and check yourself before emotions get the better of you, and you have overcome the greatest hurdle to leading a logic-based life.

We are not looking for perfection. Progress is the goal. I can tell you that this area has been especially tough for me, and it requires my attention daily! One technique I use is what I call "the pause," especially when it comes to financial decisions. Although making quick decisions is an inherent habit in the way a Cheetah operates, pay attention to when a quick decision is not essential at the moment and pause.

"Never confuse a single defeat with a final defeat."
--F. Scott Fitzgerald

CHAPTER EIGHTEEN

THE LADDER

"You do not have to see the whole staircase...just take the first step!"
--Martin Luther King Jr.

When we are born into this world, we are entitled to two things: basic nutrition and the love and care of another human being; nothing more and nothing less. Let's address the easy one first. If you lack basic nutrition, you will not survive, so we all know that everyone reading this book received at least one of those basic needs.

The second need is much more complex. What defines the love and care of another human being? The degree to which we receive the love and nurturing of another human being in the development years from birth to six years will have a profound effect on the development of a child's brain and their related challenges in life. This is a separate topic for another book by an expert in this area, but for the purposes of climbing your ladder and battling the common barriers along the way, we will assume that although it may not have been perfect, you had some level of basic love and nurturing from birth.

A few years back, I saw an interview with the legendary fighter Sugar Ray Leonard, who is worth in excess of $100 million. The host asked him, "Do you think any of your several grandchildren will follow in your footsteps?" He simply replied, "They can't; they aren't hungry. They didn't grow up hungry like me."

For those of you who were born on third base, don't think for minute that you hit a triple. You are not privileged; you're soft! As Tim Grover says, "Pressure is a privilege." Denzel Washinton once said, "Ease is a greater threat than hardship."

It doesn't matter where you come from; it's what you're made of. Earlier I mentioned that what you don't have can only help you. This creates hunger, drive, and determination. If you have been hungry once or twice in your life and then figured out your next meal, you already know the rules of the game to climb your ladder. No matter what your background, where you're from, or any hardships you may have endured, and for that matter, any free rides you got, all of us are fighting the same battle on the same playing field called life.

> *"I feel sorry for rich kids now...because they're never going to*
> *have the opportunity I had because I knew tough things.*
> *I can handle tough things; they can't."*
> --Ben Hogan

With that said, let's get this perfectly clear: No one owes you anything! Not your parents, not the government, not your employer or your family. The only person who owes you anything is yourself. As you have already learned from this book, this mindset is the only path to an extraordinary life. You must take 100% accountability. The minute you think someone or something owes you anything, you have allowed the victim mentality to emerge. Remember, if you know life is unfair, there is nothing unfair about it!

Also, remember that you are the only "you" there ever was or ever will be. Every one of us is born and differentiated with unique skills, talents, faults, and so on. Society has a way of shaping, forming, and thereby determining what's perceived as normal and what's not related to behaviors, attractiveness, and uniqueness. This leads to potential cruelty by the Snakes based on how you behave, your physical appearance, where you're from, or other anomalies that may be perceived negatively about you. In order to climb your ladder effectively, you need to avoid the Snakes and ignore the Sheep's views and opinions.

Embrace your uniqueness. I like to think about Lady Gaga's song, "Baby, I was born this way." This acceptance of yourself is the foundation of loving yourself and building that inner moral core of confidence and self-esteem. Remember, all that matters when we wake up and at the end of the day is how we feel about ourselves.

When short-term success comes your way, it is imperative that you stay grounded. Latch on to your inner core and let your principles rule your direction and actions. Remember, no matter the win, no matter the money, you are no better than any other human being, simply different.

"Keep your feet on the ground and keep reaching for the stars."
--Casey Kasem

The eternal climb

The ladder is a graphical depiction of your life. Gravity is a natural part of nature that pulls you down...it's the path of least resistance. In turn, the natural path of the ladder is downward. However, the climb up the ladder can give you an advantage if executed properly. It is based on a life span of 90 years. You may immediately ask why 90 years when the average lifespan expectancy is close to 80 years. Well, as you've noticed in this book, we are not looking for average in *anything* we do. If you play your odds and percentages in the game of life and live exceptionally, as outlined in this book, you will be anything but average. I personally plan my life and future based on 100 years.

When we look into the execution of climbing your ladder, we will break down the 90 years into various different time frames, all of which will represent one rung up the ladder measured in time. 90 years is 270 quarters, 1,080 months, 4,680 weeks, 32,850 days, 788,400 hours, 47,304,000 minutes, and 2,838,240,000 seconds. The thoughts that take place in all of these time frames, except the seconds, are conscious thoughts. Most of what takes place in the time frame of seconds are subconscious thoughts. We will explore the relationship between these time frames and what focus will propel you up your ladder in the most efficient manner.

Note that your subconscious mind has as many as 80,000 thoughts per day which approximately lines up with the 86,400 seconds in a day. Of those thousands of thoughts, 80% are negative, and 95% were exactly the same repetitive thoughts as the day before. Your subconscious mind is responsible for 95% of your brain power and your thoughts. Therefore, your subconscious mind creates 95% of your life.

We now know that the subconscious mind is extremely powerful, and that it does about 95% of the work, and therefore the conscious mind only does about 5%. You are only consciously aware of about 5% of all your "stuff" going on in your mind. The vast majority of your subconscious mind's thoughts are developed between birth and age seven.

The approach to moving up your ladder over time will be to positively and consistently reprogram or overlay your subconscious mind to tilt your micro-thoughts in a more positive direction. As we learned from the marble mind from brain power, making changes of this sort is difficult. Therefore, we are only looking to make micro changes to have a more positive outcome and move the odds and percentages a few points in our direction. The core of who you are is challenging to change, to say the least.

My approach is to be aware of your subconscious thinking so we can apply some logic to your outcomes by inputting better information. You will fight a daily battle between the primary, dominant thoughts coming from your subconscious mind versus the controllable thoughts from your conscious mind. The more you engage in the logic and discipline to get your conscious mind engaged in this battle, the quicker the results will come. At Thrive Global, they approach it this way: *You are so much more powerful than you think, so get to work. I want you to ONLY think about what you DO want and NEVER about what you DON'T want. This is also the key to manifesting. Create the pictures of what you do want in your mind, and watch how the subconscious mind and the Universe bring it for you!*

After I met Russell Anderson in the mid 1980s, I set my dreams on a Jaguar XJS coupe like the one he had. Of course, this was simply a dream until I put a picture up at my desk of the exact car I planned to get one day. It was a red V-12 with chrome wire wheels. I focused on the photo daily and literally planned out how financially I was going to make this happen. That's how you go from a dream to a goal to a commitment and execution. By 1990, that beauty was sitting in my driveway!

To illustrate the concept of the ladder, let's take a look at the stock chart of Apple. I think we can agree that Apple is one of the greatest companies of all time. Apple has made contributions to the world that changed the future of civilization for the better. Furthermore, the company created thousands of millionaires for its staff and shareholders.

However, as you can see in its stock chart, the path to greatness was not straight up. The company had tremendous failures and setbacks on many occasions and almost went bankrupt in the late 1990s. Many battles were fought on the way to the top, and many were lost. Through relentless resilience by its founders and key executives, the company rebounded multiple times after setbacks over a period of decades to emerge as an Alpha Lion of the business world.

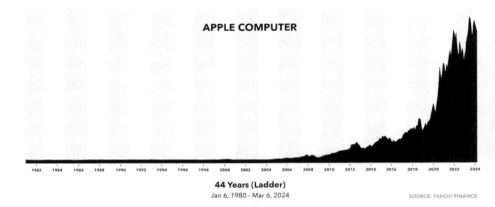

APPLE COMPUTER

44 Years (Ladder)
Jan 6, 1980 - Mar 6, 2024

SOURCE: YAHOO FINANCE

Apple Computer was founded in 1976 by Steve Jobs, Chris Wozniak, and Ronald Wayne. Interestingly, Ronald Wayne quit the company after only a few weeks due to his view of it being too risky. That was Sheep mentality. Apple went public in 1980 at $22 per share. When viewing the chart above, it appears that all was well at Apple from its inception until the early 2000s, where you can see on the chart the critical mass in growth start to take hold. However, if you could zoom in on the period from 1980-2000, as the chart depicts below, you would see tremendous volatility in the stock price as the challenges and risk of the early growth years reflected major internal flaws and external market condition impacts.

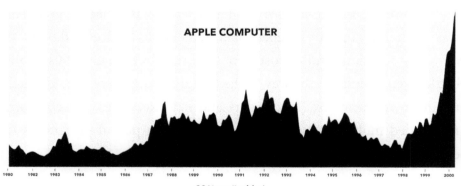

APPLE COMPUTER

20 Years (Ladder)
Jan 6, 1980 - Mar 6, 2000

SOURCE: YAHOO FINANCE

Throughout the 1990s, the company sputtered through several setbacks including product and management issues, such as:

- Heavy competition from companies like Microsoft and IBM
- Several product releases that sold poorly, like the Newton PDA
- Refusal to license its software to other companies, further limiting its competitive edge
- Too much focus on high-end products.

It took the return of Steve Jobs and an overhaul of their business strategy to save the company from bankruptcy.

The takeaway I want you to grasp is that you can correlate your life to the age of Apple. When Apple was born, it had nothing but hope and a prayer from a few visionaries with an idea. When you are young, you are the same way.

When Apple was in its adolescent years, from 15 to 25 years old, it was finding its way through trial and error, just like you have or will experience during those years.

As the company emerged through innovation and excellent management, all derived through experience over time, the foothold on the validation of the organization began to be on firmer ground, therefore being able to weather any storms headed its way. As you build your foundation and begin to shoot PARRR in your late 20s and 30s, you too will experience a stronger foothold in your life.

Now that Apple is in its 40s, it stands on solid ground. However, as you can see from the stock chart, it has had several setbacks over the past decade, some self-inflicted, and some related to outside market conditions. The setbacks are simply setbacks, not a threat to their existence or survival, and you can see on the chart that these setbacks are followed by glorious comebacks. This only comes with maturity and a seasoned world of experience. Your life, as you gain experience and maturity, will reflect the exact same way as long as you are willing to engage in the battles to make the initial climb and be prepared for all future battles. You learn to anticipate setbacks and are prepared to deal with them as a launching pad to the next level of your ladder.

My final reflection about the Apple stock chart is the macro view. The duration of the setbacks was not measured in weeks or months but were measured in years. Can you see how irrelevant the early-year setbacks were when you look at the long-term success? In fact, you can't even see those early setbacks on the first chart. However, in the midst of these early trials and tribulations, they were impactful and severe at the moment. It would have been easy to throw in the towel and quit at any one of those early-year setbacks as the task to survive in some cases seemed insurmountable. You will experience the same challenges when climbing up your ladder. Be prepared for time frames measured in years. Remember this concept when you are going through hell: many years from now, it's only a learning experience designed to launch you to new heights. As the country song by Rodney Atkins says, "If you're going through hell, keep on going. Don't slow down! If you're scared, don't show it. You might be out before the devil even knows you're there."

Note: If you invested $10,000 in Apple in 1980, it would be worth over $14,000,000 today. You can make your climb to an exceptional life as well!

Segments of the Ladder

Now it's time to build your ladder. The ladder is shown below.

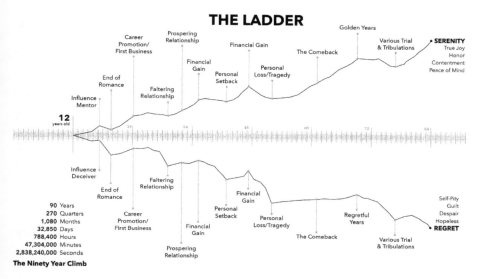

The first thing to note is the flat starting point trajectory, up until the 12th or 13th year, where we begin to take on the responsibilities and consequences of our decisions. In Judaism, at the age of 12 or 13, a child has a Bar Mitzvah for boys and a Bat Mitzvah for girls. This is a celebration of many things related to Jewish law, but for the purposes of the ladder, it is when an individual becomes an adult and takes on the moral obligations and responsibilities of their actions. Therefore, starting at a very young age, you had a direct input on the trajectory of your ladder.

Secondly, notice the tick marks along the baseline. The 90 larger marks are the years, the 270 smaller marks are the quarters, and the little marks you can barely see are the months. If you could look closer with a microscope, you would see the days, hours, minutes, and seconds, but these are not visible to the naked eye. The reason you can't see them is because, just like in real life, nothing about your growth and success is measured in any shorter time frame than months, and even this time frame rarely shows. Most successes and major leaps up your ladder are measured in years.

The concept Is to **dream your dreams but work on your goals**. That's a broad statement, but your short-term commitments, thoughts, and actions consistently applied will accumulate to a measurable longer-term result. The reason we quit is that we either simply didn't commit to a duration long enough to get a result, or we are not innovative in our resilience to pivot when facing obstacles. The upward-sloping ladder requires faith in the process and the resilience to endure through setbacks and failures, in some cases for years at a time.

The best example is someone who wants to look better and sets out to lose 30 pounds. Well, after one day of diet and exercise, do you think you magically look better in the mirror? Of course not. But you did log a win for that day and moved one step closer. Then, after 90 days, or a quarter, if you were one of the few who actually stuck to your plan, didn't cheat, and went to the gym daily, that image in the mirror will have a significant impact on your mind and your future. This process repeated thousands of times in all aspects of your life is rung by rung the climb to an extraordinary life.

Only one in a thousand successfully execute plans like the one described above because of the lack of understanding of the subconscious mind. The subconscious mind will definitely win all the battles eventually *if you let it*. Remember, it controls 95% of your thinking, so common sense will tell us that this is where we need to focus if we are going to scale up the ladder. Although psychiatrists and psychologists could write thousands of books on this topic and give detailed biological explanations for our deficient behavior and how our brains work, as you figured out by now, I like to simplify things.

As Earl Nightengale said in his famous broadcast back in the 1950s, "The Strangest Secret," "*We become what we think about.*" In order for you to move up rungs on your ladder, you must buy in and wholeheartedly have faith in this principle.

Just like the reason you can't see the shorter time frames on the baseline, you will not be able to measure the short-term changes in your thinking and subconscious mind. Again, you need faith in the long-term results of your short-term actions. Your short-term thoughts and actions are the paths to reprogram your subconscious mind. It's not actually reprogramming, it's more like overwriting the old information with new.

The old information and thoughts of the past will always remain, and as soon as you stop or pause on the consistent input of the new content for your mind, the ugly past will resurface immediately. That's why this is not a project; it's a lifestyle that challenges your discipline daily. Once you start this path, you will clearly recognize when you stopped with the positive input and the fade back to the past begins. Not to worry. This is normal and actually a huge positive factor once you can see the setback. This allows you to reset repeatedly until one day there is no going back. You know how to control it, and you will not allow it!

The Cheetah in you will be faced with peaks and valleys. There will be droughts where hunting will be scarce, and then there will be times when you are dominating the plains. In order to conquer the kingdom, you must repeatedly attack and pounce on every opportunity regardless of the environment. Remember, the Cheetah is a resilient, disciplined survivor on the prowl who will quickly change course to assure his ascent.

In my 30s and 40s, I committed over 100 times to stop eating fast food. Fast food was the daily routine with the four kids' activity schedules and my 70-hour work weeks. With each setback, there was a reset, and another reset, and yet another. Until one day, I placed my normal order of a Big Mac, Fish Sandwich, fries, and a coke, pulled up to the window, and paid. I noticed one of those drive-by trash cans just after the pickup window, and I threw the entire order in the trash! The unhealthy days of 1,800 calorie/134 fat-gram meals were eliminated after years of failed attempts.

Trashing that order was the moment of victory! I had convinced and programmed my subconscious mind to be strong enough to drive right past McDonald's, no matter how hungry I was or how good those fries smelled. My mind was controlling my emotions. It's been 20 years since I ate a Big Mac, and I don't miss it a bit!

Here's another example. I engaged with self-learning and growth when I was in my late 20s. As time passed, my confidence grew, and my success in business soared, I started to get away from all the things that got me there in the first place. I thought I did not need this anymore. I had made it.

Well, you know what happened from my mid 30s to low 40s from my story. This period of time was a major setback on my ladder. However, knowing what led to my previous success, I re-engaged in the daily processes of self-learning and physical fitness that launched me originally, and magically, again, I was on a good trajectory. The same theme applies; the comeback is always greater than the setback!

Once you have been there to that place of glory, you can get there time and time again regardless of getting off track, even if there are years in between. Now, my self-learning, health, and physical workouts are the baseline of my existence. I know if I allow any of these areas to falter, I'm headed right back to the demons of the past. It's imperative that you find your non-negotiables within yourself that will hold you like glue to your principles, no matter how difficult the task, circumstances, or challenges facing you.

Focus Four: Changing your short-term thought processes
Success requires a relentless focus on the minutes,
hours, and days while maintaining complete faith in
the months and years. Are you ready for this battle?

Now that you understand the end game and the general premise of how it works, let's dig into making this happen. Most people wonder where their thoughts come from, or why their thoughts are so negative. You will never solve any of your negative thought processes by awareness and mental correction alone.

Changes in thinking come from actions and results. Overwriting your subconscious mind comes from regimented, disciplined *actions*. Dreaming about being a millionaire or having an amazing marriage or a multimillion-dollar business will do nothing to change your subconscious thinking. Those dreams will go to the grave with you without consistent commitment to short-term actions. Look at it this way: you cannot climb a rung of your ladder that's a mile away in one step. To execute the influence on your subconscious mind, we will focus exclusively on the shorter time frame rungs. I call these the "Focus Four."

The Nano Rung (Seconds)

Welcome to your subconscious mind. There are 86,400 seconds in a day, and our minds produce as many as 80,000 thoughts per day. When we think in terms of time frames of seconds or less, our subconscious mind is virtually 100% in control of our thought processes. Therefore, you will not consciously try to change the thought process for this time frame. You will use the next three rungs to influence the nano-rungs that will control your climb. As you positively impact the minutes, hours, and days, the nano thoughts entering your brain will begin to change. This is the end game of your future. We know that the average human processes their overall thoughts as a percentage of 60% negative. We are going to aim to tilt those over years of time to 60% positive! Nothing will impact the quality of your life more positively than this process and its end result.

The Micro Rung (Minutes)

Now, we are moving to the conscious mind. Right now, this very minute, you have decisions to make! Ask yourself, "What am I doing now, and what am I going to be doing a minute from now?" Sounds elementary, but if your actions right now and one minute from now are not actions that yield benefit to a daily win you are continuing to reinforce and negatively program your subconscious mind. Therefore, if you take steps down in the micro rung time frame, it will result in steps down in the nano rungs. This is counter to the process of positively influencing your subconscious mind.

These are little actions like hitting the snooze, not flossing, or stopping your workout 10 minutes early. Pay attention to your very short-term thought process. These add up throughout the day and will leave you not only with a negative impact on your subconscious mind but also with a loss for the day and a rung down on your long-term ladder. The longer you decide to take micro rungs down, the more difficult it will be to develop the pattern of daily wins that propel you up your ladder. Everything Counts!

The Mini Rung (Hours)

Now that you understand your short-term micro focus and thought process, there are two things to propel you up your mini rung. First, start planning your day by the hours. If you're not writing it down, at a minimum, plan in your mind what your day looks like by the hour. Have a conscious plan of attack and try to regiment your day by the hour. No, I do not expect you to be a robot and have every minute 24/7 accounted for. This is a general guide to holding yourself accountable. Sure, build in your escape time and allow for a little time for nothing, but the majority of your time needs to be accounted for and related to the actions of goals, projects, and commitments. Furthermore, you need to be the General in Command. This planning process will reflect back to your nano rungs in that just the planning itself will inject positivity into your subconscious mind.

At the end of each hour, ask yourself, "Was that hour a win or a loss?" Give me the majority of your waking hours with recorded wins, and I'll show you a winning day. This keeps the ladder moving upward. Everything Counts!

Often, if we get off to a bad start, we admit defeat for the day, or we consistently fade in our discipline as the day moves on. For example, most people have difficulty disciplining their diet after 6 pm. A trick I use to counteract this is what I call the Triple Challenge. I divide the day into 18 hours: 6 am-12 noon, 12 noon-6 pm, and 6 pm- midnight. Imagine a 6-hour ladder. My goal each day is to get a triple win. However, if I lose one, I start over with the next one. Breaking this down will allow you to recover midday instead of throwing in the towel for the day. Your 6-12 pm shift will be your most challenging as your mind gets tired and your discipline fades. Challenge yourself to win the battle of the toughest hours, the night shift!

The Core Rung (Days)

Tomorrow is another day? No, it's the *same* day unless you change your actions!

Your daily rung should be envisioned as a rung on a standard ladder. It's called the Core Rung because it's the easiest time frame to measure your results. Make this a non-negotiable *core* of your climb. Your nano, micro, and mini rungs accumulate throughout the day to add up to one daily core rung. Did you take a step up or a step down today? With each rung up, the view gets better!

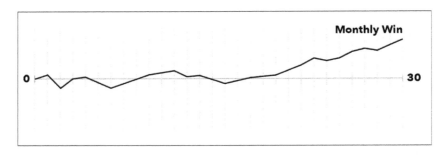

Monthly Ladder - 30 Days

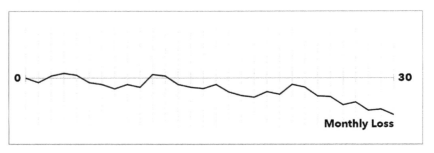

Your daily goal is to execute on all of your shorter-term rungs consistently to propel you upward. There will be setbacks. When you have a down rung day, as your last thought before going to sleep at night, tell yourself, "Okay, it's just a one-day minor setback; I'll reset and relaunch in the morning."

Sell this to yourself consistently. We all have off days, and just like everything else we discussed, you are looking to improve the trend over time. We are simply looking for more up days than down days, so your trend line is sloping up to the right. I recommend you inventory your daily rungs. Make your own graphical chart of your ladder and plot your daily progress across the month. At the end of the month, is your core ladder higher or lower? The accumulation of your daily rungs is the core of the ladder and will yield the long-term ultimate goal of complete serenity.

The longer time frame rungs are not achievable without the Focus Four rungs. In order to climb a weekly, monthly, or yearly rung, you must combine an accumulation of daily rungs to get there. No one can step up a ladder where the rungs are miles apart but rung by rung, day by day, the miles are achievable.

As we discussed in the execution of the ladder concept of "everything counts," both positive and negative, your goal is through mini, micro, and nano thoughts and actions to compile daily wins. Daily wins turn into weekly wins, then monthly and yearly. What will magically happen is that your subconscious thoughts will begin to change as you move through this process. You do not need to be conscious of this process, you simply need to engage in daily actions and activities that change your immediate thoughts. Get so busy that you do not have time to be depressed. Over-commit and leave no blank space on your schedule except your planned escape time. The more your mind is engaged in your immediate activity, the more positive programming you will be doing.

It's not just about what you do to input the positive focus four actions in your mind, it's also about what not to do. The attack plan to engage in your battle needs to address the negative short-term actions you are engaging in daily. Just like the Focus Four rungs that I described to take proactive, positive actions, you absolutely must begin the process of eliminating the negative Focus Four. These are subconscious thoughts that keep you in negative daily habits. The best way to do this is to replace the negative actions/thoughts with a positive action/thought. Eliminating the negative input is just as important as enforcing the positive, if not more so.

Remember, highly successful people do not engage in detrimental behaviors of any kind. Let's say you are a casual pot smoker on the weekends. This is clearly an action that will move you down a rung on your ladder. Replace this with another activity, sport, or hobby. I prefer physical activity so you can get a little dopamine high to replace the feeling of relaxation or escape. This one simple change, if you make it permanent, will build your confidence and launch you up the ladder. With each negative eliminated, your momentum will surge. Nothing easy here; remember, it's a battle. Now imagine replacing five or ten negative inputs with positive actions!

The Sheep's Demise:

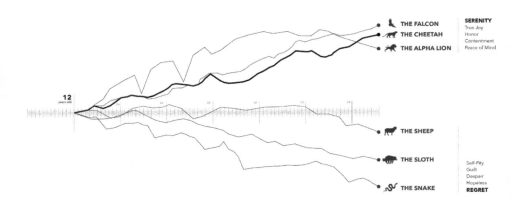

As you can see on the ladder, the Sheep hangs around the baseline and will spend the majority of their life above the baseline with occasional dips below due to "woe is me" behavior and the random setbacks that life throws their way. Remember, Sheep do not have bad intentions like Snakes but are held back from their climb due to their conforming mentality, lack of confidence, and the inability to take risks. Sheep can be wonderful people, but I view them as misguided. Therefore, they hold themselves back from accelerating up the ladder like a Cheetah.

"Well," you may say, "I am not interested in being a Cheetah, and I enjoy my Sheep-like lifestyle. I am perfectly content with that."

My response is, "Content, yes, but for how long?"

As Sheep approach the later stages of their ladder, they begin to dip below the baseline because they realize that they did not go after or pursue life up to their capabilities and potential. Regret creeps into their mentality, and a feeling of "it's too late" goes to the grave with them. They feel guilt, despair, and sadness. These feelings are hardly what any of us ever want to experience in our senior years. I urge you to bet on yourself now and get engaged. Your most precious commodity, time, is ticking away! You know the alternative.

Again…Faith in the process

Embedding positivity and upward steps into your being takes years. This perspective and deep understanding are vital to developing your resilience and not quitting. As you can see, in the typical ladder, whether you are a Cheetah or a Sheep evolving into a Cheetah, most of the glory of your efforts that create lasting inner joy is not fully realized until the decades of the relentless climb have been achieved.

This is why it is imperative to learn to love the battle and the climb along the way. You will spend decades in various trials and tribulations as you climb. So few people understand this, and it's why most of us are doomed to a Sheep lifestyle. We all quit repeatedly, way too early, resulting in the negative feedback loop and acceptance of "I guess that this all there is to life."

I am here to tell you, do not cut yourself short of your potential! You are a unique being that, in my view, can and must make the climb to an extraordinary life. Being a Cheetah is a lifestyle, not a project. The Cheetah in you will sprint all the way to the grave.

What's the alternative?

*"Hell on earth would have been to meet
the person you could have been."*
--Tony Robbins

CHAPTER NINETEEN

SERENITY

Many of us are dead before we die.
Do not allow this to happen to you.

Now that we have worked our way through the process of climbing your ladder to an extraordinary life, let's settle in to take a look at the ultimate destiny we all seek. At various stages of our lives, and along the climb, we become engaged in obsessive periods of behavior related to our age, wants, desires, and goals. Without those obsessive behaviors, the climb would not be possible. You will experience extended periods of time without balance in your life, so stop seeking it.

All of this is normal as you mature from adolescent to adult, taking on life's evolution of responsibilities of marriage, family, and profession. Throughout this period, most of us seek to gain not only emotional stability but to accumulate things as a reflection of our efforts. We reward ourselves with homes, nice cars, and material items that confirm to ourselves the worthiness of our efforts.

I'm in no way against accumulating nice, comforting things in life. Material goals certainly drove my actions, aspirations, and motivations when I was in my 20s, 30s, and 40s. How you accumulate material things is an important endeavor that should only be acquired with cash flow streams from other investments, but that is a conversation for another book. Whether you want an exotic car collection, private flights, and a $3 million-dollar home, or you take Warren Buffet's approach of living in his parents' house and driving a 20-year-old car, it's a choice that's individualized to your personality and what makes you tick. So, to each his own. My brother, who built his 100-million-dollar company, takes pride in being somewhat of a minimalist, whereas my wife and I like to enjoy nice stuff.

Regardless of the approach, the trials and challenges you endure during your growth years will begin to wane when you reach your 60s, as you transition into a Falcon or a mature Cheetah.

> *"Real wealth is having something money can't buy."*
> – Brad Lee

You will realize that time is your most precious commodity and learn that all of the most valuable things in life cannot be bought. This is when serenity becomes a part of your existence. You begin yearning for the intangible, reflecting on the most precious things you have experienced in life like graduation day, your wedding day, your first child being born, building a snowman with your grandchild, the dogs you owned, the person you saved, or the people you launched to a better life.

You will start to value your relationships more and see the goodness in people differently. Drama will dissipate as you learn that it's simply not worth your time or energy. Haters will have no impact on you. You will take pride in the success of the children you raised and the quality of the humans you put on this earth. Your love for your life partner will continue to grow as the two of you reflect on the world and family you built together. You will look at each other like the day you met for eternity, reflect on the empire you built together, and each of you will know you were the lucky one. Grandchildren will be the joy of your life. The best description I've heard of this place called serenity is "Silent Harmony"...it's an inside job.

It's obvious that nothing on the list above could be bought, so although I do believe that money is an important part of freedom and your ability to help others, it's not an absolute requirement to reach the top rungs of your ladder. However, most of the time, money chases the Cheetahs, Falcons, and Alpha Lions.

"You will never regret gratitude, but greed will get you every time."
--Justin Freishtat

The Five Horizons – Health, Family, Finances, Profession and Faith
Without a vision, our dreams will perish!

Throughout this book, you have heard repeatedly that all growth and success come from short-term thoughts and actions, as explained in the Focus Four. I also said to dream your dreams but work your goals. Furthermore, I said that if you do not yet know your "why," you should focus on your "how."

The reason you may not know your "why" yet is because it lies on a distant horizon. You may not yet have met the spouse of your dreams, built your multimillion-dollar business, started your family, or embarked on your journey of discovery. We all know it's fun to fantasize about winning the lottery, so let's apply the same concept of the Five Horizons to visualize your life 30, 40, 50 years from now.

What does that picture look like? Although your visualization may be a fantasy today, it will not be decades from now. I would like you to spend some of your escape time visualizing and fantasizing about what you will become decades down the road. This can take place before bed, or you can do as I do and visualize during workouts. Through this process, you may find your "why," or at least evolve toward it.

I guarantee that this time will come, and it will arrive sooner than you can anticipate. Do you see yourself as a wealthy, healthy, fit person who is the leader of your family with loyal allies? Knowing the path you will take is not as important as the visualization that, yes, you *will* be there one day. Look at your future for all five horizons: health, family, finances, profession, and faith.

If you do not look out at your five horizons and see the potential for yourself, you will end up being the same you that you are now 50 years from now.

Visualizing yourself on these horizons will help you internalize the big picture as you execute everything you learned in this book. What you see out on your horizons will help reinforce your discipline, accountability, and integrity as you climb up your ladder. Furthermore, visualizing your horizons is fun, inviting, and uplifting.

The last of the horizons is faith. If there is one thing I hoped I convinced you of, it's to have **faith in the process**. All high achievers embrace this like a religion. Faith is a big leap for many due to the nature of the ladder and life's setbacks. I urge you to develop unwavering faith that, over decades, if you maintain your inner moral core and discipline yourself to execute your way up the ladder, you will become the exceptional person that you were put on this earth to be.

The strong, resilient heart

> *"Where ashes fall, legends rise."*
> --Godsmack

I've often wondered what makes the difference between people who become victims of their circumstances, acting out of desperation, and those who use those circumstances to reset, grow, thrive, and overcome adversity. Who rises out of the ashes after they fall? Who steps up versus hanging in the back of the crowd?

We all face random, inexplicable events. Some of us embrace unfairness and approach all randomness in life as fair because we know it's eventually coming and we are prepared. As I said earlier, there is nothing unfair about life if you *know* it's unfair.

Most of us have experienced "the call" that we never thought we would get, completely unexpected, where we learn news that may be devastating or even tragic.

I've experienced these types of crisis calls multiple times in my life. I got the call from a friend telling me the news that confirmed with certainty that my marriage was over; the call to learn I had lost millions in a scam; and the worst call of all came when my youngest son, who had a newborn and 2-year-old, called crying on the phone, to tell me he had leukemia.

My response and reaction have changed over time as I have climbed my ladder. You know that my divorce story drove me into complete victim status for almost two years, but the comeback had a profound effect on my inner strength and resilience moving forward.

When I got the call just a year ago about my son, I immediately slipped into that same victim mode again. Of course, as any parent would be, I was crushed with panic, pain, and heartbreak.

However, after about 48 hours, I reached deep down into my soul and used my experience to tell myself that it was time for leadership and action. I quickly moved into action to do everything possible to save my son's life.

My wife and I spent the next month doing research and consulting with my son and his wife on a daily basis to find the best doctors and facility to win this battle. I discovered that my previous experiences to hell and back made me unbreakable. I felt empowered. Unbreakable does not mean completely shutting down your emotions. Believe me, there was lots of crying and much-needed hugs during this period, but the ability to execute in the toughest of times lets you know the pinnacle you have reached internally.

I was able to lead and be the father my son needed instead of being weak and falling victim to feeling sorry for myself as I had 25 years earlier. After my son went through a year-long battle of intense treatment, I got the best call I'd ever received, telling me that he was cancer-free. He won that hard-fought battle so he can go on in life being an exceptional husband and amazing dad to his two young children.

You cannot explain the randomness in life, but you can build your inner core of resiliency to become unbreakable. Your willingness to embrace the battles of fear, risk, pressure, doubts, and insecurities and throw yourself into the arena to compete repeatedly is your path up the ladder to becoming unbreakable. The strongest hearts have scars. In order to execute this, you will need to leave the Sheep herd and run with the Cheetahs! This is why working on yourself is the greatest gift you can give to others. Becoming unbreakable is the path to serenity.

A tribute to Mom and Dad
We want to die with memories, not dreams.

As I write this book, my parents have celebrated their 70th wedding anniversary. They are both in their early 90s and have clearly reached complete serenity in their lives. They have more than sixty grandchildren and great-grandchildren.

My mother was one of five children. Her mother, my grandmother, came to the United States alone as a teenager from Lithuania in the early 1900s. A relative had enough money to get one member of the family out of what was a terrible situation enduring widespread poverty. She had three sisters and two brothers, all of whom were left behind.

About a decade after she left, World War II was on the horizon, and the Nazis came into town. They rounded up all of the Jewish families – women and children included - and machine-gunned them all down like cattle in the street. Her entire family of brothers, sisters, and all of their children were exterminated in an instant. She was the only survivor of her generation. My grandmother had a profound impact on my mother and her sisters, impressing on them the blessing of being in the United States of America. My grandmother made sure that my mother and her sisters would never be victims of the family history. She imposed the opposite approach on my mother by building a new life with the opportunities she and her sisters created as they grew up.

My mother and her four sisters are responsible for putting over 200 quality human beings on this earth. What a tribute to my grandmother, who was the last surviving member of our family...from one survivor to 200 descendants! And I might add that all 200+ are people of the highest integrity and character.

My father was the son of immigrants from Ukraine and Belarus who came to the United States in the 1920s with nothing more than a suitcase and a dream. Where you come from has a lot to do with the gratitude you exhibit and the thankfulness for opportunity.

The pride my grandparents had just to be Americans and live in a land of opportunity affected me deeply. My grandparents lived a life of paycheck to paycheck, but family was their real wealth. My brothers and I were blessed to have loving and caring parents who would never be victims of their past.

There were plenty of tough times growing up as we, too, lived check to check, just like the generation before us. Even though money was always tight, my brothers and I never felt like we missed anything because not only our immediate family but the extended family was close. Again, it wasn't stuff or luxury vacations that made my childhood so memorable, but it was the relationships and experiences my parents created with cousins, friends, and extended family. And then, as you heard in my parents' story earlier: they took a big risk to build a better life for us, and the Cheetah was unleashed!

"Instead of buying your children all the things you never had, you should teach them all the things you were never taught. Material wears out, but knowledge stays."
--Bruce Lee

Ed Mylett, speaker and author, talks about being "the one." By this expression, he means the one in your family who makes that generational shift to a better life and passes it down to their children. When you are teaching your kids, you are also teaching their kids. My parents became "the ones." Are you going to be "the one?"

You have no choice but to live an exceptional life. Unleash the Cheetah!

"Be the change you wish to see in the world." - Gandhi
What's the alternative?